Library of Contemporary Architects

RICHARD NEUTRA

Library of Contemporary Architects

RICHARD NEUTRA

Introduction and notes by
RUPERT SPADE

with 86 photographs by
YUKIO FUTAGAWA

SIMON AND SCHUSTER NEW YORK

All rights reserved
including the right of reproduction
in whole or in part in any form

Copyright © 1971 by Thames and Hudson Ltd, London
Photographs copyright © 1969 by Yukio Futagawa

Published in the United States by Simon and Schuster
Rockefeller Center, 630 Fifth Avenue
New York, New York 10020

First U.S. printing

First published in Japan in 1969 by Bijutsu Shuppan-sha, Tokyo, in their series
GENDAI KENCHIKUKA SHIRIZU.
New texts have been provided for this English language edition.

SBN 671-21055-6
Library of Congress Catalog Card Number: 77-159582

Printed in Japan

Contents

Introduction 7

The Plates 21

Notes on the plates 123

Chronological list: projects and events 131

Select bibliography 133

Index 135

Introduction

In the closing chapter of a now famous book,[1] Reyner Banham observed that the pioneers of the Modern Movement, working prior to the Second World War, fundamentally misunderstood the nature of technology; they imagined that the dynamic process of technological evolution, whose first stirrings so greatly enthused them, was destined to end swiftly in the establishment of a new vocabulary of classic forms and methods expressing the nature of the new machines. In this they were mistaken. As Banham has pointed out, performance soon made it necessary to pack the components of these machines into a streamlined shell. Comparisons between automobiles and the Parthenon—such as were made by Le Corbusier in 1923—became less and less convincing as the century advanced and the form of automobiles themselves changed. By 1939 the static, vertical composition of the elementary vehicle of 1923 had become the horizontal dynamic composition of a record-breaking Mercedes or a Bugatti Atlantic coupé.

The visual link with technology was broken: the form of trailer homes, prefabricated bathroom units, domes and space-frames further obscured the connection. After 1945 a positive avalanche of conceptual and material products, spun off from the massive technological output of the Second World War, swept the elementary formulations of the pioneers of the 1920s to one side.

How could one continue to observe 'truth to materials' when new synthetic materials supplanted natural ones every day? How could form follow function when function had become elusive and mutable instead of self evident and permanent? How could the 'shape' of technology be deduced from a violently evolving system of forms which seemed to possess a taxonomy of its own?

As for the development of media—of instantaneous electronic communication, of computers and other installations whose cost far exceeded that of the buildings erected merely to *enclose* them—how could a form, a shape and a meaning be appended to these? Functionalism under these conditions degenerated into mere mechanical expressionism: its capacity to hold the seething forces of technological change within the grip of a theoretical matrix already a quarter of a century old became at first strained, then overstrained, and finally collapsed.

The pioneer architects of the modern movement reacted variously to this overrunning of their theoretical camp. Some, insulated by age and personal success from any kind of general vulnerability, went on reiterating the slogans of the past and built according to images firmly fixed in their pre-war experience. Others more enterprisingly abandoned the moralistic basis of functionalism altogether, and leaped instead upon the sheer multiplicity of new technological phenomena—detecting therein a whole new system of meanings within which a designer might construct a revolutionary cosmology. A third group, more concerned with the practicalities of influencing those concerned with fabrication of the expanding human environment, strove to provide a foundation in the life sciences for those intuitive slogans and tendentious projects which had served as theory in the past.

Probably the most distinguished of this last group was the *émigré* Austrian architect Richard Neutra. He feared something immeasurably worse than the fate of architects left behind by the march of technology. 'Humanity,' he stated in 1954, 'appears now at the mercy of a rampant, over-advertised industrial technology which is flooding us off our psychological bearings and threatening to drown the entire race like a litter of defenceless kittens.'[2] Here, the declension in tone—from concern that architecture had taken a wrong course to doubts about the future of humanity—is instructive. Neutra's Jeremiad has gained in relevance in the sixteen years following (until the time of his death in 1970) and the stoic calm of his conceptual framework shows signs of increasing rather than diminishing in importance. He once wrote prophetically:

> 'When we are lucky and feel strong, we want to take things firmly into our hands, plan ahead, even arrange the most distant future. When we are stricken by sickness, loss, and failure, our plans shorten desperately. Then they are reduced to the next week, the next day. During a heart attack we only plan for a mere second or two—for reaching the chair in front of us.'[3]

Richard Neutra was born in Vienna in 1892 into a family whose father had risen from mould-maker to joint owner of a brass foundry. By his own account[4] he discovered a love of smooth surfaces on the floor of his parents' living room, digging out dirt compacted between the floorboards, tasting it, and pronouncing it 'no good'. His concept of height and scale dated from the same juvenile experience, for he recalled having rejected the high ceiling of the living room in favour of the underside of the grand piano, beneath which he would sit and play for hours. In the fullness of time the young Neutra grew up and enrolled at the Vienna Technische Hochschule where he came under the influence of Otto Wagner and, later, Adolf Loos. These two quite dissimilar men had a lasting effect upon Neutra's thinking, and memories of both stayed with him until his death.

The work of Wagner—the older of the two—had impressed Neutra even during his childhood—when he would run backwards and forwards through the Municipal Railway stations designed by him.

Loos, on the other hand, influenced Neutra in more profound ways. A powerful polemicist—largely through lack of work—Loos had developed an intense dislike of ornament as well as an extravagant respect for what he termed 'classic forms', such as carved oak lavatory seats and bicycles. His doctrine of 'lastingness' in architecture, as a direct rejection of any principle of style or fashion, stayed with Neutra all his life, and there is more than a trace of Loos' famous 'ornament is crime' in the first paragraph of Neutra's *Survival through Design*:

> 'Nature has long been outraged by the design of nose rings, corsets, and foul-aired subways . . . ever since Sodom and Gomorrah, organic normalcy has been raped again and again . . .'

However his admiration was not fulsome; writing as late as 1966, Neutra recalled that even in 1910—when Loos was forty years old and he was eighteen—he had been sceptical of the older man's polemic. By 1923, when Loos submitted his famous competition entry for the design of the *Chicago Tribune* building (this featured an immense skyscraper in the form of a Doric column), he confessed to being 'perturbed'. Nonetheless the influence of Loos' *personality* he judged to be permanent. Reviewing Munz and Kunstler's biography of Loos, Neutra confessed to almost feeling a true plagiarist of Loos, because 'personality impacts, integrated and fused, are more important than any kind of formal borrowings and loanings.'[5] This insight is particularly valuable, for it explains why Loos the Americanophile was more influential with Neutra than was Loos the architect of the unadorned Steiner house of 1910—one of the canonical buildings of the modern movement in Europe.

Loos, who had been to America during the early 1890s, working his passage, struggling as a stonemason, but not achieving even the status of draughtsman in an architect's office, had nonetheless seen the best of Sullivan's buildings in Chicago and, much more important, had returned with a clear insight into the immense industrial and technological potential of the New World—and of a new, pure architecture grown from its machinery. This vision he succeeded in conveying to the student Neutra during the weeks he spent working in the architect's office on a project for a department store. With the publication in Germany of the Wasmuth edition (1910) of Frank Lloyd Wright's work, Loos' tales seemed triumphantly vindicated. Like Rudolph Schindler, his near contemporary at the Hochschule, Neutra resolved to emigrate to this 'fantastic living culture of some yet unknown people'.[6] Schindler obtained work in America in the summer of 1914 and left Vienna before the outbreak of war. Neutra was not so lucky, he spent three years as an artillery officer in the Imperial Austrian army before finally taking his degree *cum laude* from the Technische Hochschule. In correspondence with Schindler, then working for Frank Lloyd Wright, Neutra endeavoured in vain to find a means of getting to America but, with the collapse of the Austro-Hungarian Empire in 1918, he fled to Switzerland where he worked for the landscape gardener Gustav Ammann. The two years he spent there taught him a great deal about plants, trees and the whole quality of the site upon which a building stands, lessons which he was later to put to good use in his own domestic buildings.

By 1921 he had left Switzerland for Germany where in the disturbed conditions following the end of the war he worked for a time in the town of Luckenwalde resettling city workers in rural dwellings. 'By living with my patients,' he observed later—using the medical analogy which always came easily to him—'I took my own medicine.'[7] In the same year Neutra paid a visit to Erich Mendelsohn in Berlin where the latter, to the accompaniment of Bach recordings, was sketching an extension to the offices of the *Berliner Tageblatt*. Starting as draughtsman, Neutra swiftly became Mendelsohn's partner and in 1923 the pair won first prize in a competition for the design of a business centre in Haifa; but the project was never executed. Germany, in the year of massive inflation and of the Munich *Putsch*, was not the place to get any project executed.

Towards the end of 1923 Richard Neutra, without his Swiss bride Dione, left for the United States. From being draughtsman and partner to the one-man firm of Erich Mendelsohn, he was exposed for a year to the office of 1,328 draughtsmen at the Detroit firm of Hinchman and Grillis. 'The original founders of this firm were dead, and the five new ones who drove me around Detroit were also dead.'[8] Later on he became draughtsman No. 216 at the firm of Holabird and Roche in Chicago. These gigantic planning factories did, however, provide him with material for a book on American building methods, *Wie Baut Amerika*, which was published in Stuttgart in 1927.

At the same time as he was earning an anonymous living in Chicago, Neutra made the acquaintance of the aged and ruined Louis Sullivan. Their association was short, for Sullivan died in the spring of 1924, but it was at his funeral that Neutra met Wright and thereafter spent several months at Taliesin North. Wright was in his mid-fifties and at the time had reached a hiatus in his career:

> 'In Chicago he was pretty well hated. The *Tribune* retold the number of marriages he had had, and how often he had not paid his rent ... I thought it's just as if one would report on a Beethoven anniversary all the places where he didn't pay his rent. This revered, sad man invited me to come to Taliesin. My wife had stayed in Europe, and when she gave birth to a little boy, we called him Frank! Soon she brought this boy and even my mother-in-law to join us.'[9]

In the following year Neutra moved west to California, he shared a house and an office with Schindler—whom he had not seen for ten years—and the pair jointly worked on projects for a civic centre for Richmond and the international League of Nations Secretariat competition: neither entry was successful. Finally, after working on a large urban project of his own called 'Rush City Reformed', which featured pedestrian/vehicle segregation, a population of one million, and a remarkably Brasilia-like appearance, he obtained sufficient commissions to establish his own practice, first with the 1927 Jardinette Apartment building, and later with the famous 'Health House' in Los Angeles—a commission awarded by Dr Lovell, a former client of Schindler's.

The 1928 Health House marked the commencement of Neutra's international reputation and also the beginning of the heroic effort to integrate the innumerable products of American technology into a single frame of reference which was mentioned at the beginning of this introduction. Esther McCoy describes thus the veritable celebration of novel technique that the construction of the house involved:

> 'The open steel skeleton, in which standard triple steel casement windows were integrated, was fabricated in sections and transported by truck to the steep hillside site. The light steel floor and ceiling joists were electrically welded before delivery and all shop

work was held to decimal tolerances to avoid costly changes on site. As a result the entire skeleton was erected in forty hours—too fast to photograph the various stages of assembly.[10]

The balconies of the house, which have the appearance of cantilevers, were in fact suspended by steel cables from the roof frame. Its walls were cast *in situ* using ready-mixed concrete pumped through hoses to cover expanded-metal reinforcement itself backed by insulating board used as permanent shuttering. This technological *tour de force* was not however achieved at the cost of the quality of the site, for it was in his unique ability harmoniously to integrate machine construction with natural surroundings that the architect excelled. As he noted in a book published in 1951:

> 'Before destruction by civilization, Nature, its objects, its constellations of stars or landscape, its natural sites, were regarded as animated. Like human faces they had a physiognomy which conveyed a recognizable and expressive message. They were thus evaluated. The promontorial rock past which the natives rowed was occupied by a spirit. A tree or a spring housed a nymph, and a certain individually characterised valley, or isle off shore, was the homestead of a God or the playground of a devil.'[11]

Neutra bemoaned the passing of this animistic oneness with the world and hoped that physiology, *Gestalt* psychology, anthropology and other nascent life sciences could restore it. He believed that a site, no matter how small, produced a 'combined total impact . . . hard to gauge, to analyse or to exhaust in its effectiveness.'[12] And in the cliff-hanging integration of the Lovell house and its successors he endeavoured to express the kind of union of building with site which in his view represented the only possible response of a sensitive architect to the divisive and destructive forces at work within the world's most industrialized society.

The Health House was widely publicized and brought in its train more work and professional success of another kind. In 1930 Neutra returned to Europe as an American delegate to the Brussels conference of the CIAM. He revisited Germany and spoke at the Bauhaus; in the Netherlands a prominent industrialist, C. H. Van Der Leeuw, presented him with a large cheque to continue his researches into house construction; in Vienna his second book *Amerika* was published with considerable success. He returned to California via Japan where a portfolio of his work was also published in the same year. On his return he was invited to design a 'Pullman of the Road' by White Motors, but the project did not materialize. Instead he concentrated on the design of an experimental house to be financed by the Van Der Leeuw cheque; this building, the V. D. L. Research House, erected near Silver Lake in Los Angeles (where a number of Neutra and Schindler houses now stand), involved far-reaching experiments on a very modest budget. Like Frank Lloyd Wright, whose cheap 'Usonian' houses began to appear a little later, Neutra saw that the old dynastic architecture of Europe, and the rich man's architecture of America, were equally inappropriate to a consumer age; new dispositions of wealth and sources of money had taken command.

'Clients are not just a few people who want their penthouses decorated or their beach houses built in nice shapes. They are not only capricious television stars with spending money, but also, for example, city fathers who dispose of staggering tax revenues extracted from all of us . . . for speedway systems, city halls, schools, projects for hundreds of thousands of families, plans to develop entire regions, states or nations.'[13]

Neutra's efforts, from the success of the Health House in 1929 to the Nesbitt house of 1942, were mainly directed towards devising a complete system of human settlement which could not only absorb increases in population without environmental catastrophe, but also provide for the great majority conditions of arcadian grace such as had previously only been accessible to the privileged few. During the Depression and in the years of the 'New Deal' which followed it, such an ambition was shared by many. In the United States, with over ten million unemployed, mortgage foreclosures running at nearly a quarter of a million every year, and the Architectural League of New York buying advertising space to urge owners of vacant property to offer it for housing to 2,500 unemployed and destitute architects, such dreams were the stuff of radical politics—as the brief rise of such organizations as Technocracy[14] clearly indicated.

With the advantage of hindsight it is possible for us to see that the failure of Neutra's 'Rush City Reformed', Wright's 'Broadacre City'—even Le Corbusier's earlier 'Ville Radieuse'—as universal panaceas did not derive so much from their *naiveté* as from the uncontrollable pluralism of American and indeed Western society itself. During and after the Second World War, when utopian thinking and political power were for a time closely interlinked, numerous developments closely related to each of these schemes were completed in Europe and America. To be sure, universal application was nowhere achieved, but enlightened patterns of settlement were more widely accepted than ever before.

The scale of the problem had however been misunderstood by the pioneers: influenced more by upbringing and class attitudes than they would like to admit, they could not see that the utopia they so vigorously propounded was at best a middle-class dream. In 1950, when a record number of 1,400,000 house completions was achieved in the United States, one third of its population was still living in unfit housing. By 1970, the year of Neutra's death, fully 40 per cent. of American families earned too little to be able to step on to the first rung of the ladder of house purchase.

At the time of the architect's earnest researches into the technology of building these grim statistics were still in the future. Nonetheless he was conscious of a certain inadequacy in the conceptual framework within which he and others worked; a difficulty in convincing those not already convinced. Even as he researched the potential of new materials he began to devote more and more time to studying the findings of psychologists, animal physiologists, anthropologists; any and every exponent of that area of human endeavour concerned with the effects of environment on behaviour and vice versa. He was developing his own ideas on the subject, striving to secure a confirmation of his work outside the uncontrollable market forces of the technologically peerless America which had so excited Loos some forty years before. He was

determined to be vindicated in the broader context of the life sciences—
by means of a design theory of his own.

For the moment, however, there was a period of technological exploration. In the V.D.L. Research House he exploited the limited potential of a very small plot (60×70 ft) by building to the setback lines authorized under Californian building conditions not yet codified. McCoy describes the house as follows:

> 'A standard wood frame is carried by precast concrete floor joists, which permit wide openings without the cost of steel framing. The main block of the house, two stories high, is joined by a hyphen to a one-storey section, with a protected garden between. The decentralised plan has two living rooms and two kitchenettes ... Electrically operated sliding glass panels make the informal garden-living room part of the patio.'[15]

The V.D.L. Research House was built for occupation by Neutra and his own family, which by 1933 numbered three sons; he also used it as his office. It was destroyed by fire on the night of 21 March 1963, but afterwards rebuilt with minor modifications by the architect and his second son Dion, who became his collaborator after 1942 and is now continuing the practice. One of the most interesting of these modifications was the replacement of destroyed shade trees by vertical aluminium louvres—a method of modulating the influx of light and heat from inside to outside which the Neutras employed extensively on public buildings after 1960, after first introducing them in the famous Kaufmann 'Desert House' of 1945.

Steel walls in prefabricated sections were employed on the 1936 California Military Academy, and in the following year on the Beckstrand house. Neutra used aluminium-coated steel—then an untried product—on the Sternberg house, enclosing a curve-walled patio by this means. He also adapted sheet-metal flooring units to serve as partition walls in the Beard house of 1935—with the result that he was awarded the Better Homes of America Gold Medal for that year. Further experiments involved the use of precast panels made from 'Diatomaceous' earth containing high-density deposits, such as is widely found along the Pacific coast.

The concept of prefabricated housing greatly interested Neutra, and his earliest project along these lines was the 'One Plus Two' expandable house of 1926, which employed tension cables and precast marine-aggregate panels. Later designs for 'one-off' houses were always completed with half an eye on the possibility of machine production, but in no case was this achieved. Like most other experimenters in the field—in Europe as well as America—Neutra was doomed to disappointment by the construction industry's inability to adapt itself to entirely new methods.

Even the overriding necessities of the war were insufficient to launch an industrialized house-building industry capable of survival under competitive market conditions. In the year of Neutra's death the United States Housing and Urban Development Administration was still eagerly awaiting the launching of a systematically organized housing industry as a result of 'Operation Breakthrough', a government-financed attempt to introduce new technologies into the housing effort. First proposed by Buckminster Fuller in 1927, industrialized housing has persistently failed to emulate the success of industrialized automobile production. Indeed, at the time of the Depression the United States Steel Corporation, after an heroic effort to market steel houses, stated that the prefabricated house was as impractical as an all-rubber automobile: all the ingenuity of architects and designers since then has failed to prove them wrong.

The Nesbitt house of 1942 marked a change in Neutra's emphasis on advanced technology. Condemned by war shortages to employ only non-strategic materials, he designed a simple dwelling in redwood, common brick and glass. The glass was the key element. From 1942 onwards —except in the case of low-cost wartime housing executed for the Federal Republic Housing Administration—Neutra concentrated on transparency in all his domestic structures. Privacy was achieved by planning; interior and exterior merged; the site entered the house and vice versa. Visually the barrier between inside and outside was deliberately distorted by outrigged columns, sometimes called 'spider's legs', and butt-jointed plate-glass windows. The kindly Californian climate provided abundant vegetation (to give privacy) and obviated the need for insulation by massive external walls-the defensive overtones of the front door were lost altogether.

The theory underlying this openness and oneness came from Neutra's previously mentioned studies in the life sciences. He had developed over a period of years a quasi-science of his own called 'Biorealism', or biological realism: the adaptation of structure to the biological realities of those who must use it. Neutra saw this basic theory in evidence throughout the natural world where plants, animals and other creatures survived by adjusting themselves to change over long biological ages. He saw also that such a time scale was no longer available to man because of the pace of his technological evolution was accelerating at such a rate that no assimilation of change was possible. In environmental terms the proliferation of unrelated, and ultimately mutually destructive, systems was in fact already poisoning the planet, 'toxic influences penetrate from them into us every day, every hour, every fraction of a second.'[16]

Combined with this general theory of incoherent technological advance was another aspect of Neutra's thinking, dating from his friendship with Adolf Loos: a hatred of ornament and fashion as deep—if not as virulent—as that of his mentor. Neutra saw the rapid changes of style and fashion as counter-productive to the whole synthesis of physiology and environment brought about through 'Biorealism'. As far as he was concerned the relegation of architectural design to the enforced triviality of fashion not only made nonsense of his own 'diagnostic' approach, but also flew in the face of economic realities—particularly as regards amortization. In the last interview he gave before his death[17] he observed 'I am very much for fashion in mini-skirts and ladies' hairdos but the most expensive hat I ever bought my wife didn't pay off in 35 years.' He also quoted approvingly the story of a client of Loos' sending the architect a second fee after 25 years because his austere, style-less house did not require replacement as did more 'fashionable' residences of similar age.[18]

Biological realism in its ultimate phase embraced all aspects of human engineering; Neutra foresaw the use of drugs, transplants, exoskeletons and many other integrative technologies designed to close the gap between organism and environment. 'The entire terrestrial scene has become a human biotope,' he observed,[19] and went on to explain that two-dimensional zoning ordinances were no way to control factories, offices or supermarkets. Instead he concentrated on a vision of *enclosed* cerebral and physical activity. In later public buildings 'photo-electrically controlled louvres compensated for the movement of the earth and the fluctuations of light level outside. Phrases like 'carefully eased working hours' escaped his lips, as did extraordinary images of a future working world.

> 'In the future the most fantastic nervous and cerebral activities will be induced and carried on with greater facility. They will be carried on, not with sweating brows, but with some inner biochemistry in the human cerebrum, which will continuously supplement the automation that does the neck work.'[20]

During the last twenty years of Richard Neutra's life he and his son Dion received more commissions than previously. The Moore house, (1952), in the dry and dusty Ojai valley, probably represents the apogee of their achievements in domestic architecture. Here all the elements so carefully developed over the preceding quarter of a century are effortlessly combined in an integrated yet open and indeterminate structure standing on water, which both cools the house and provides for irrigation. In the area of educational buildings he had already achieved considerable success prior to 1940. His Biorealistic theories were eagerly accepted in the field of primary education, initially because the light, open-sided structures he proposed were earthquake resistant, but later because the whole pattern of informal, open-air schooling which he advocated was seen to combine easily with the Californian climate and the growing emphasis of contemporary educational theorists on project-based learning. Almost forty years after he designed it as a project, the architect's 'ring plan' school, which employed individual detached classrooms ranged around a large elliptical playground, was eventually constructed at Lemoore, California, as the Richard J. Neutra Elementary School.

For a number of years after 1949 Neutra was in partnership with Robert Alexander, and numerous large-scale projects were executed jointly—including the United States Embassy in Karachi, Pakistan, and the Lincoln Memorial Museum at Gettysburg, Pennsylvania. Urbanism also occupied the partnership during the 1950s with a ten-year master plan for the island and free port of Guam (where an indigenous population of 30,000 had to be peacefully combined with an initially enormous American service population), and with the eventually abandoned Elysian Park redevelopment in Los Angeles. The latter project involved relocation problems of a type similar to those previously encountered by Neutra in Germany shortly after the First World War had ended.

The collapse of the partnership with Alexander led to the formation of a final arrangement with his son Dion which lasted until Neutra's death. During his last years he travelled extensively, spending long periods in his native Vienna death. During his last years he travelled extensively, spending long periods in his native Vienna. He died in Wuppertal, West Germany, on 16 April 1970.

1 Reyner Banham, *Theory and Design in the First Machine Age*, London, 1960

2 Richard Neutra, *Survival Through Design*, New York and Oxford, 1954

3 Ibid.

4 Ibid.

5 *Forum*, July/August 1966, p. 88; review of *Adolf Loos* by Munz and Kunstler

6 Esther McCoy, *Richard Neutra*, New York, 1960, and London, 1961

7 Ibid.

8 *L'architettura*, No. 181, Rome, November 1970; Neutra obituary issue

9 Ibid.

10 McCoy, op. cit.

11 Richard Neutra, *Mysteries and Realities of the Site*, New York, 1951

12 Ibid.

13 Richard Neutra, *Survival Through Design*

14 Technocracy was a political organization which flourished in the United States between 1929 and 1933. It consisted largely of unemployed engineers who announced that in the event of the Depression worsening they would set up an engineers' dictatorship to govern according to scientific principles. Franklin D. Roosevelt's 'New Deal' forestalled them. See R. Buckminster Fuller, *Utopia or Oblivion*, 1966

15 McCoy, op. cit.

16 Richard Neutra, *Survival Through Design*

17 *L'architettura*, No. 181

18 *Forum*, July/August 1966

19 Introduction to *Survival Through Design* (second edition, paperback), 1969

20 *L'architettura*, No. 181

21 Chemstrand carpet advertising feature (*Forum*, 1968)

The Plates

Photograph by Schmoelz-Huth, Cologne

1-10, The Health House (Lovell house), Los Angeles, Calif. (1929)

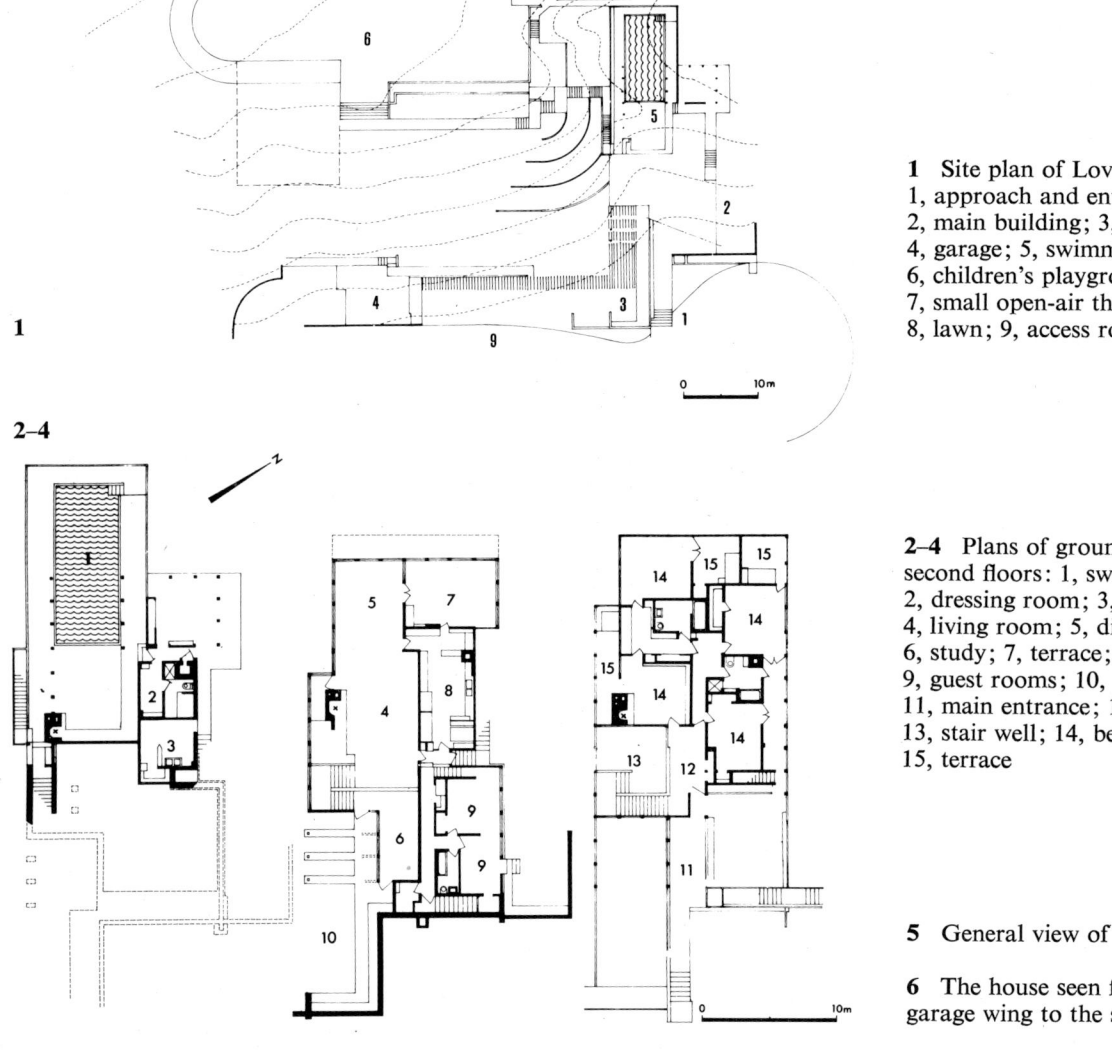

1 Site plan of Lovell house: 1, approach and entrance; 2, main building; 3, patio; 4, garage; 5, swimming pool; 6, children's playground; 7, small open-air theatre; 8, lawn; 9, access road

2–4 Plans of ground, first and second floors: 1, swimming pool; 2, dressing room; 3, laundry; 4, living room; 5, dining room; 6, study; 7, terrace; 8, kitchen; 9, guest rooms; 10, patio; 11, main entrance; 12, hall; 13, stair well; 14, bedrooms; 15, terrace

5 General view of Lovell house

6 The house seen from the garage wing to the south

7 Main entrance

8 Entrance to lower level

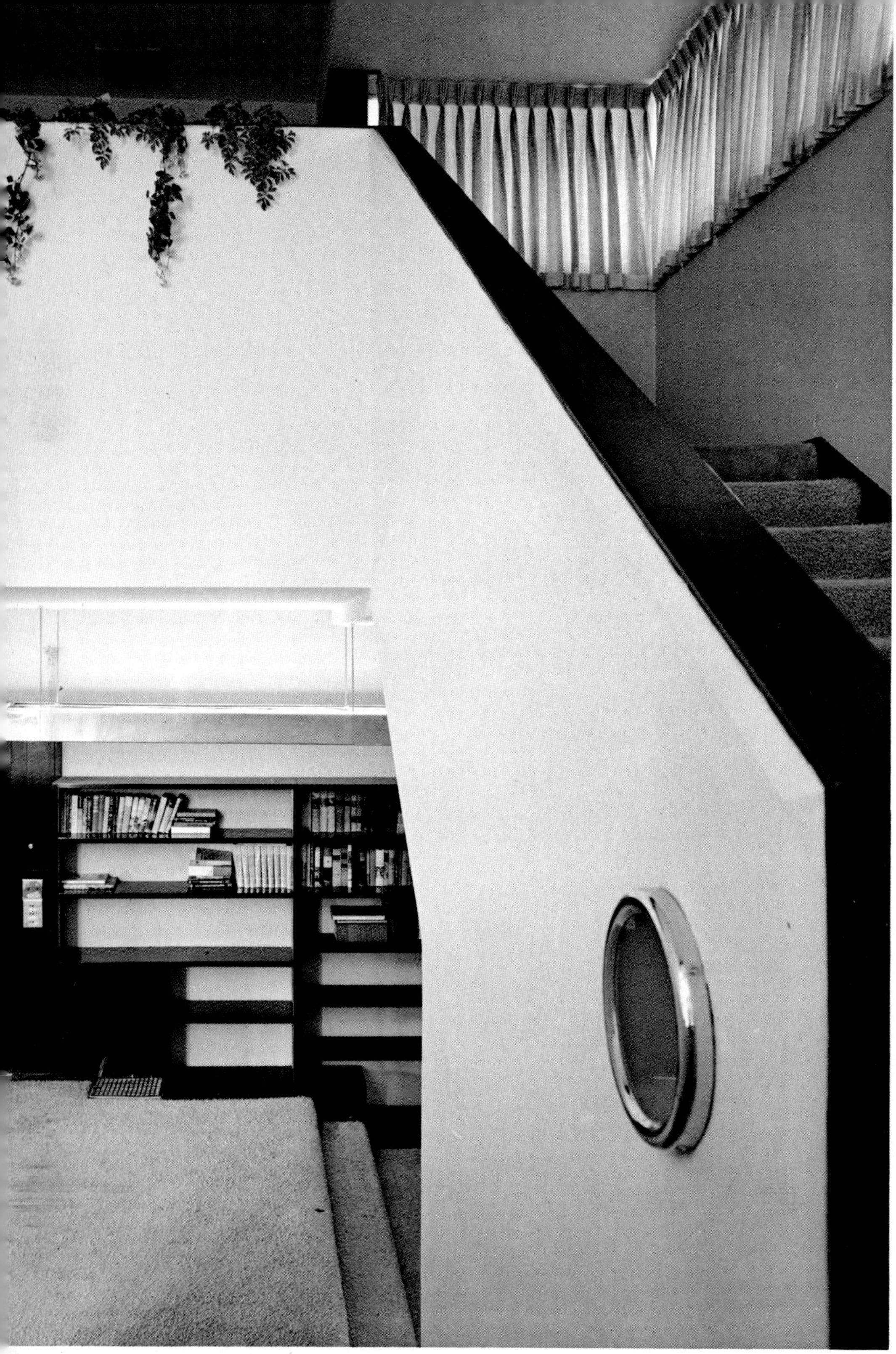

9

10

9 Stair well

10 Living room seen from foot of stairs

11-17. The Josef von Sternberg house (Ayn Rand house), San Fernando Valley, Los Angeles, Calif. (1936)

11 View from the entrance drive to the west of the house

12 Mirrored bathroom on the first floor

11

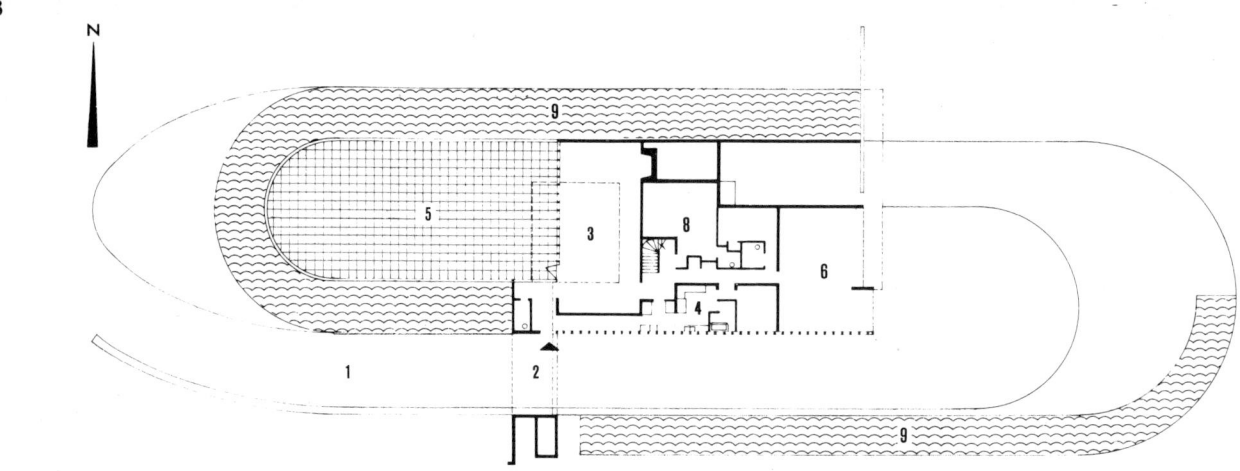

13 South side of house beyond entrance bridge; the moat is in the foreground

14, 15 Plans of ground floor and first floor: 1, drive; 2, main entrance beneath bridge; 3, living room; 4, kitchen; 5, west patio; 6, garage; 7, bedroom; 8, studio; 9, moat

16 Second floor with light-well

17 Living room showing open well to first-floor level

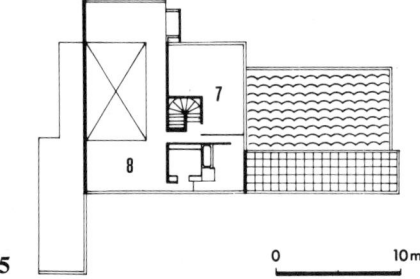

16

17

18-22, The Beckstrand house, Palos Verdes, Calif. (1937)

18 The living room

19 The west elevation seen from the garden

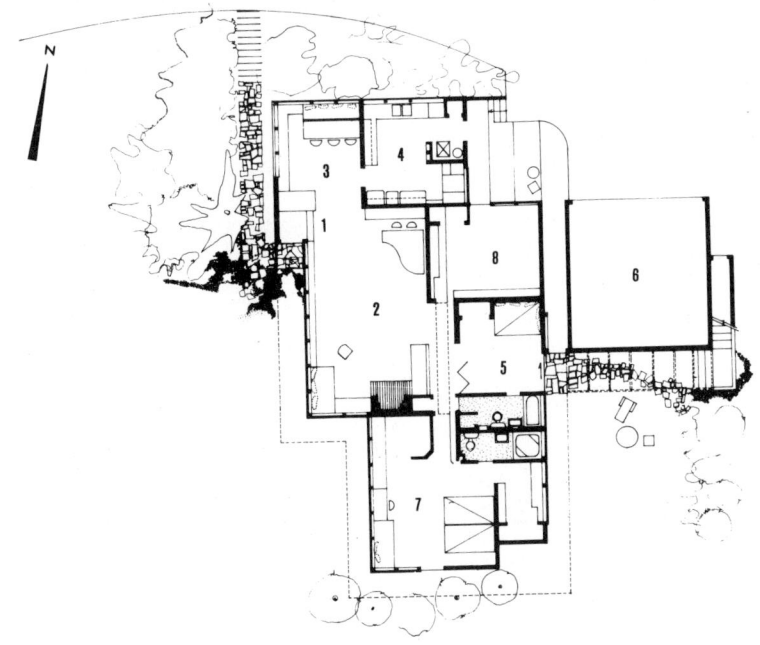

20 Plan of the Beckstrand house: 1, entrance; 2, living room; 3, dining room; 4, kitchen; 5, guest room; 6, garage; 7, bedroom; 8, study

21 The living room looking west; the view extends to the Pacific ocean

22 The dining room; the furniture is not original

**23-29, The Kahn house,
San Francisco, Calif. (1940)**

23 General view of the house from the east. The living rooms are on the top floor

24 View of the house from the lower slopes of Telegraph Hill

25 Main street entrance

26 View from the north showing street entrance

27–29 Plans of basement, ground and second floors: 1, entrance; 2, hall with staircase and lift; 3, living room; 4, kitchen; 5, terrace; 6, garage; 7, breakfast room; 8, studio; 9, bar; 10, living room; 11, workroom; 12, butler's quarters

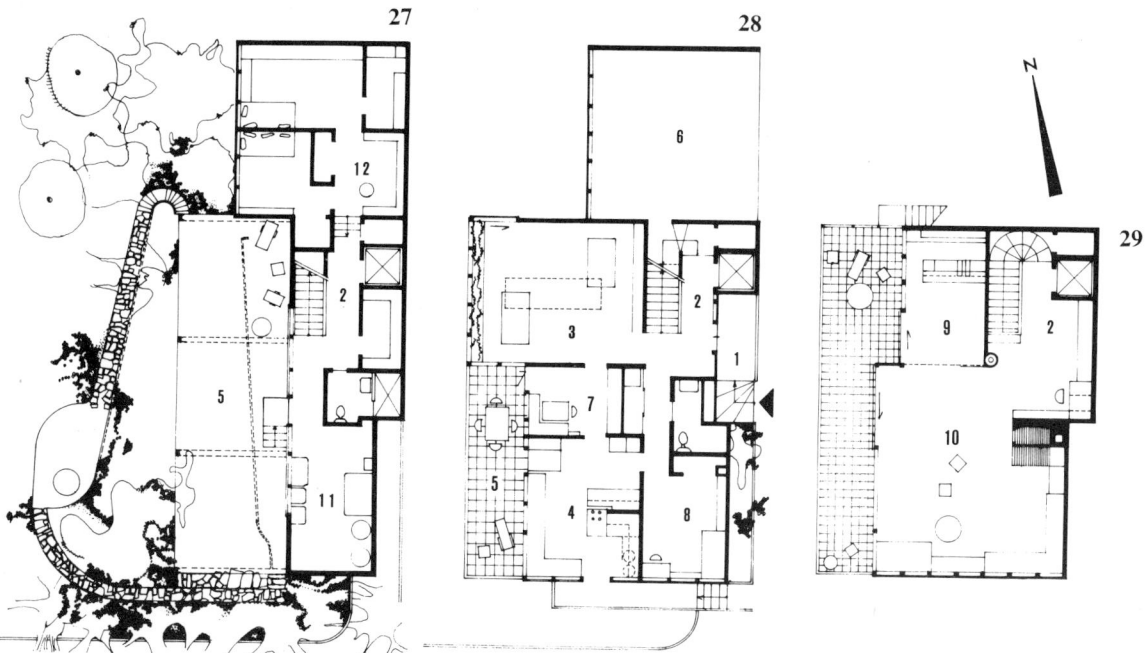

26

27 28 29

30-35, The Nesbitt house, Brentwood, Los Angeles, Calif. (1942)

30 The west elevation, with garage to the left

31 General plan of the house: 1, entrance porch; 2, living room; 3, dining room; 4, kitchen; 5, terrace; 6, garage; 7, guest bedroom; 8, guest living room and studio; 9, swimming pool

32 Living room and garden seen from the entrance

33 Living room and garden

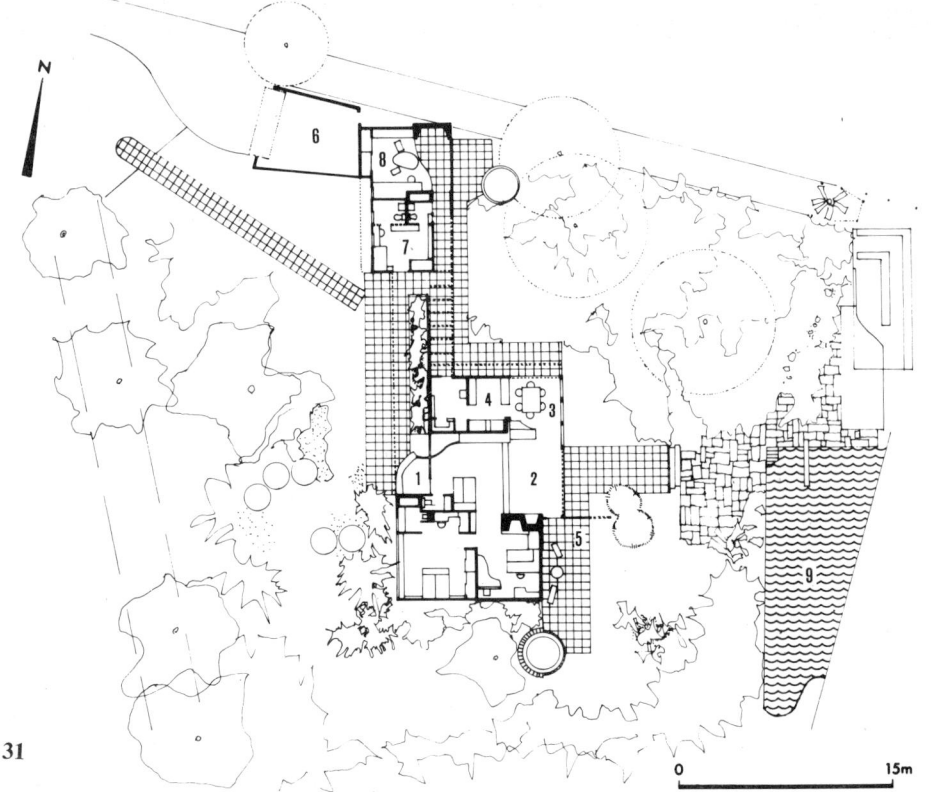

30

32

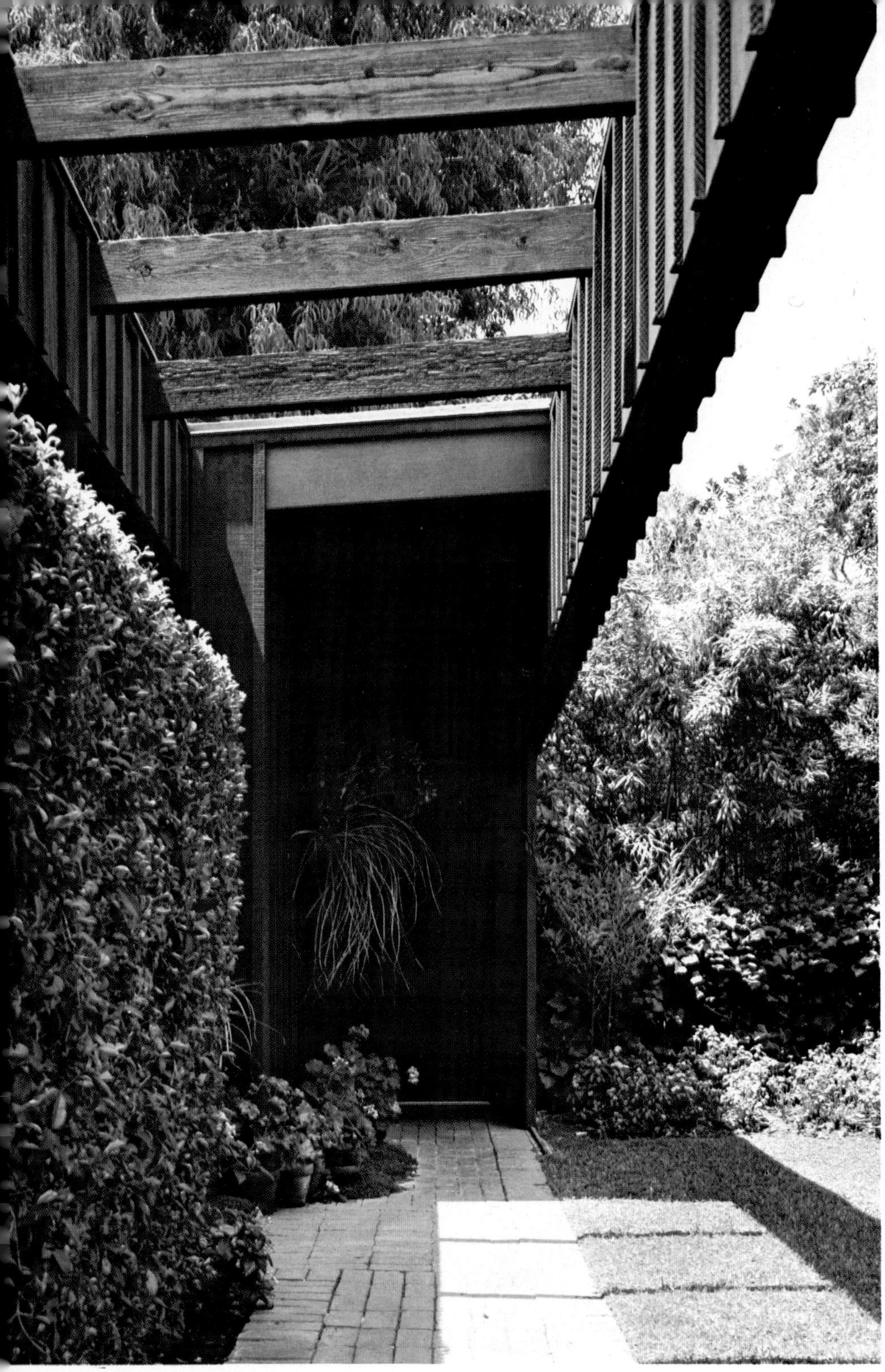

34

35

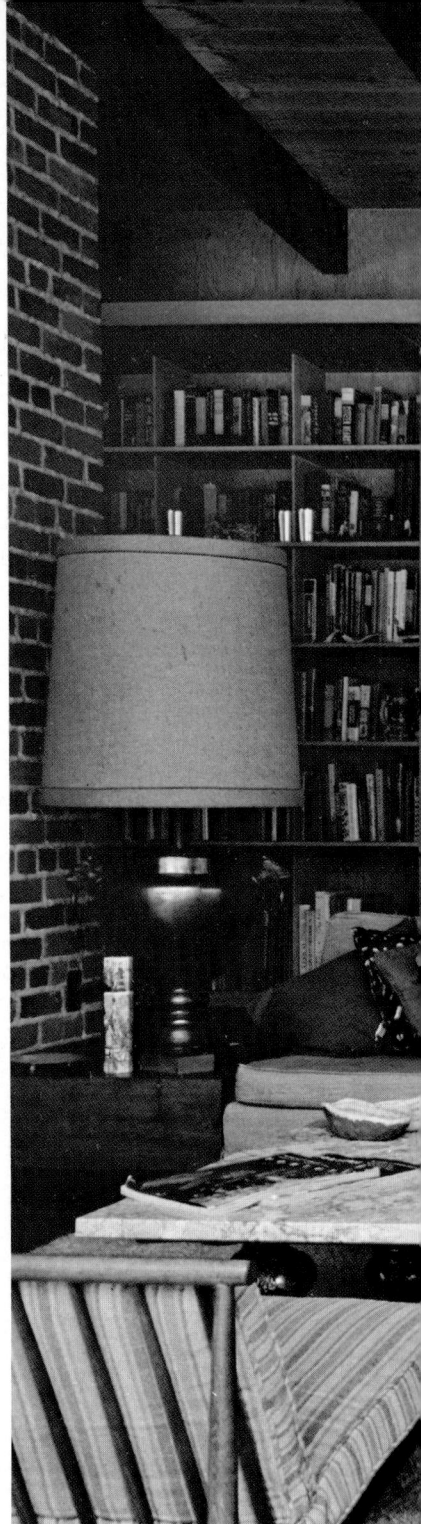

34 Entrance to guest house from main house

35 View from the sunken living room towards the entrance

36-42, The Kaufmann house, Palm Springs, Calif. (1945)

36 Ground-floor plan:
1, entrance; 2, living room; 3, dining room; 4, kitchen; 5, patio; 6, garage; 7, bedroom; 8, guest rooms; 9, swimming pool; 10, servants' quarters

37 Entrance path, with garage wall partially obscured by vegetation

38 Living room and first-floor sun terrace

39 The house from the east, with treeless hills beyond

40 View of the pool and garden from the outside staircase

41 View towards pool from the living room

42 Bedroom, with swimming pool beyond to the right

40

41

42

43-48, The Tremaine house, Santa Barbara, Calif. (1948)

43 Swimming pool viewed from the terrace

44 Main entrance, with guest room to the left

45 Dining room and corridor with translucent screen

46 Interior seen from the entrance, with the living room to the left

47 Ground-floor plan:
1, entrance; 2, living room; 3, dining room; 4, kitchen; 5, terrace; 6, garage; 7, bedrooms; 8, guest room; 9, swimming pool; 10, servants' quarters

48 Corridor from dining room (used as play area)

46
47 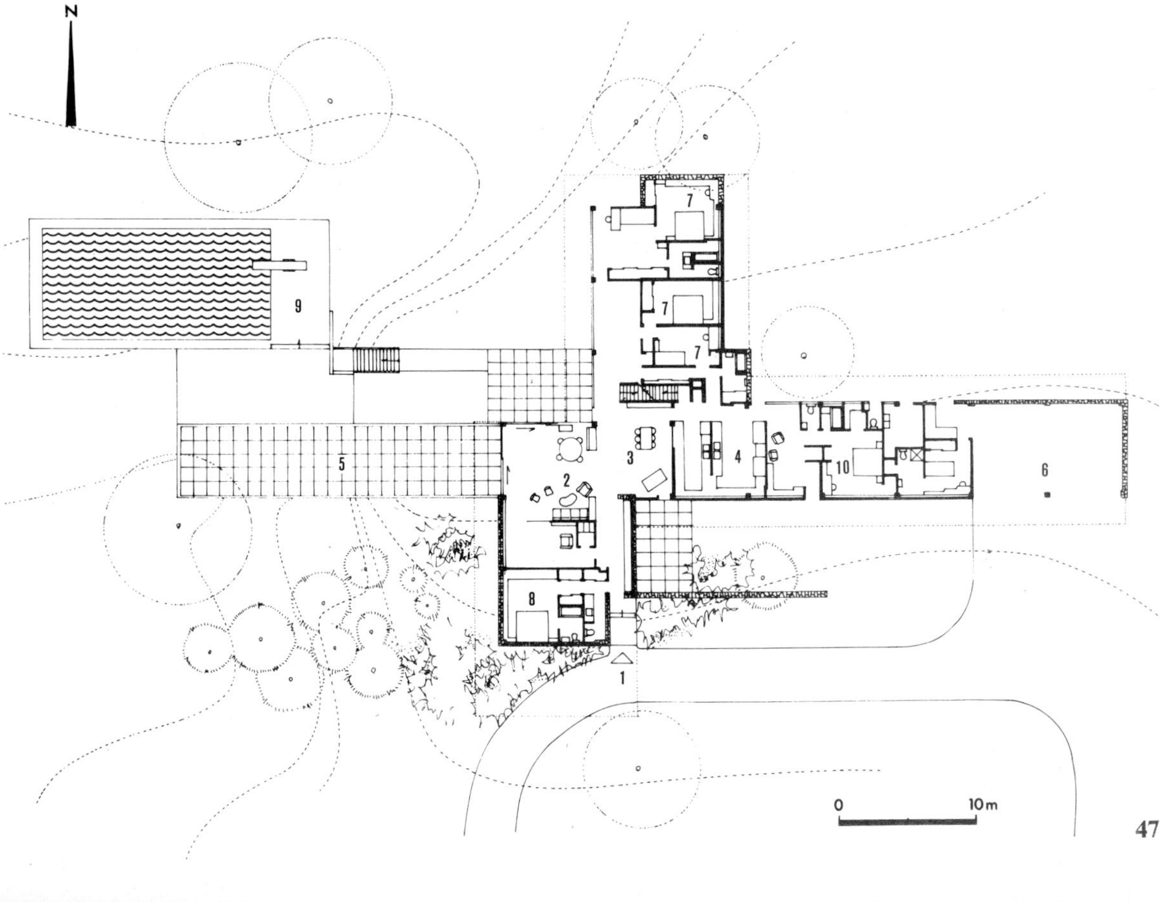
48

49-53, The Haefely-Moore twin houses, Long Beach, Calif. (1950)

49 Plans of the Haefely-Moore twin houses; the Haefely house, with stair to the bedroom over the garage is the lower of the two. Key: 1, entrances; 2, living rooms; 3, studies; 4, kitchens; 5, courtyard; 6, garages; 7, bedrooms; 8, swimming pool; 9, common entrance passage

50 Entrance to the Moore house seen from the north

51 Common entrance passage, showing timber loggia

52 The living room of the Moore house, showing false ceiling in redwood

53 View from the living room of the Moore house on to courtyard, showing dividing wall to ensure privacy

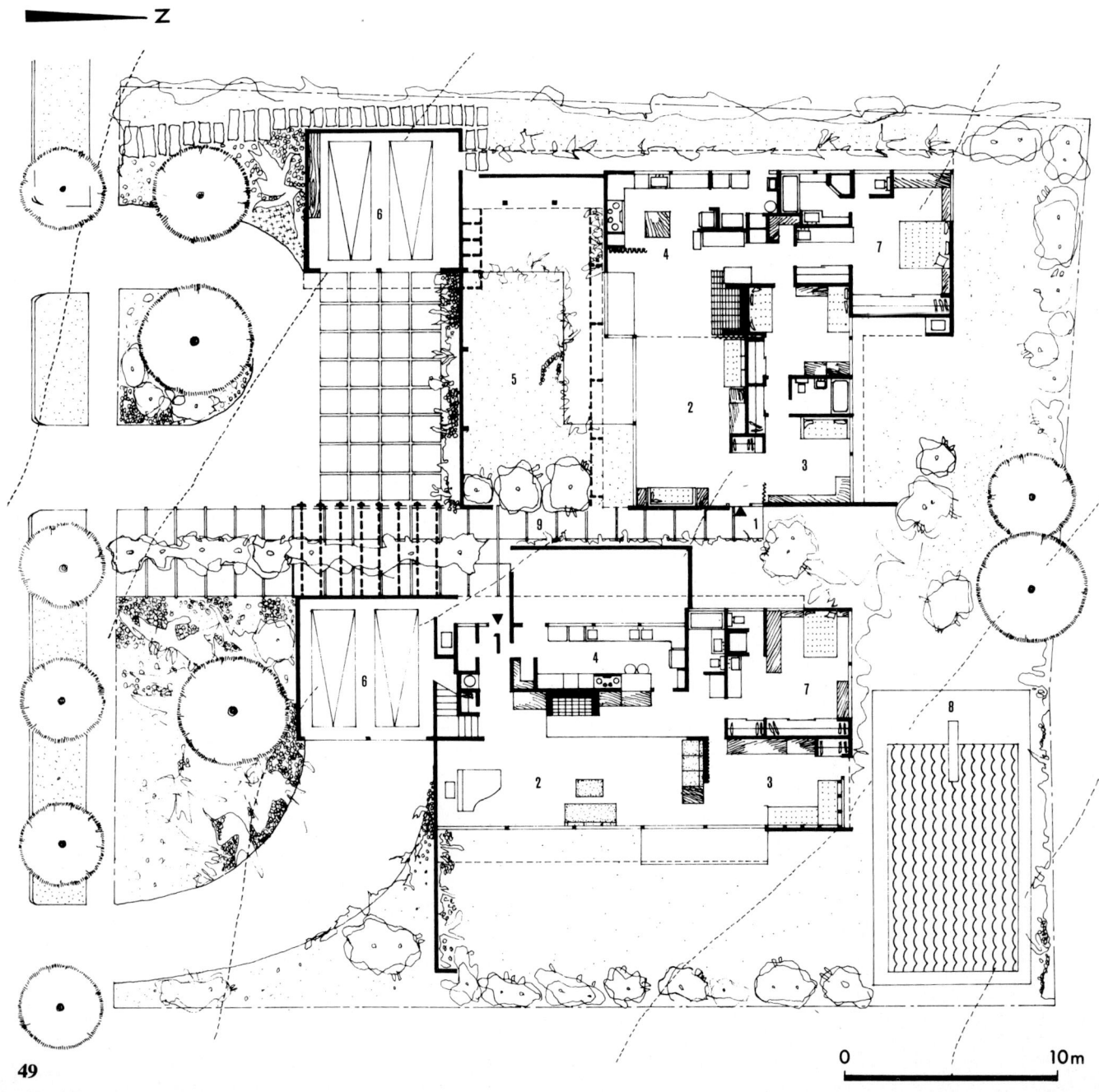

50

51

54-57, The Moore house, Ojai, Calif. (1952)

54 East elevation of the living area showing outrigged column rising from the pool

55 Terrace at north-east corner

56 Site plan of the Moore house: 1, stone-flagged entrance path; 2, living room; 3, dining area, completely glazed; 4, kitchen; 5, loggia; 6, garage; 7, bedrooms; 8, dayroom; 9, pool; 10, separate guest house

57 Outrigged column and beam, with terrace beyond

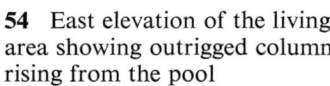

55

56

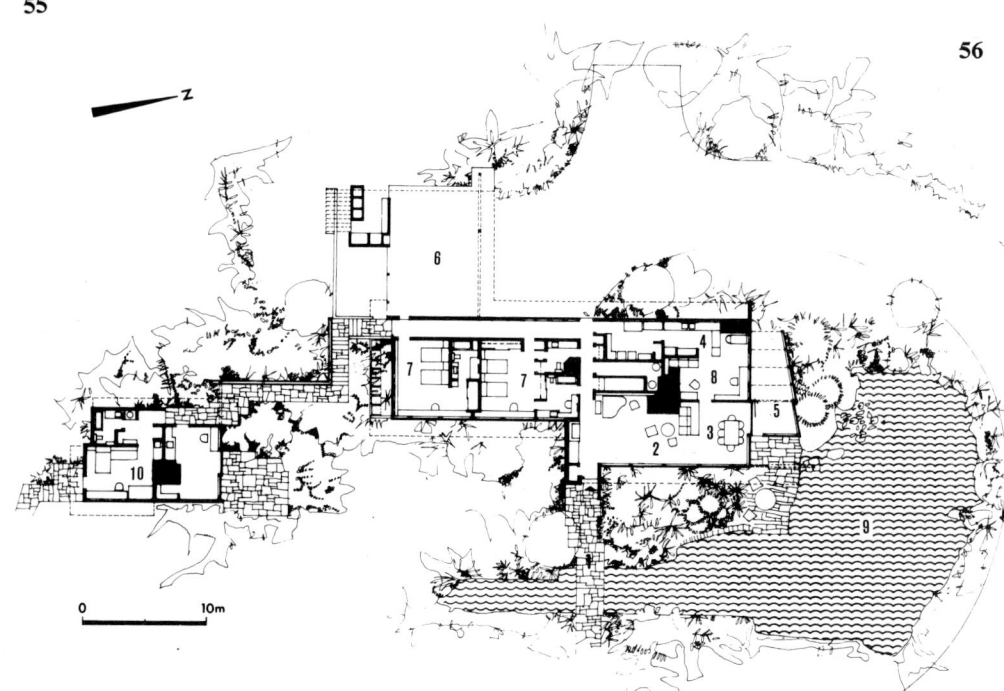

0 10m

58-61, Eagle Rock Playground Club House, Los Angeles, Calif. (1953)

58 The elevation to the east, with gymnasium in centre

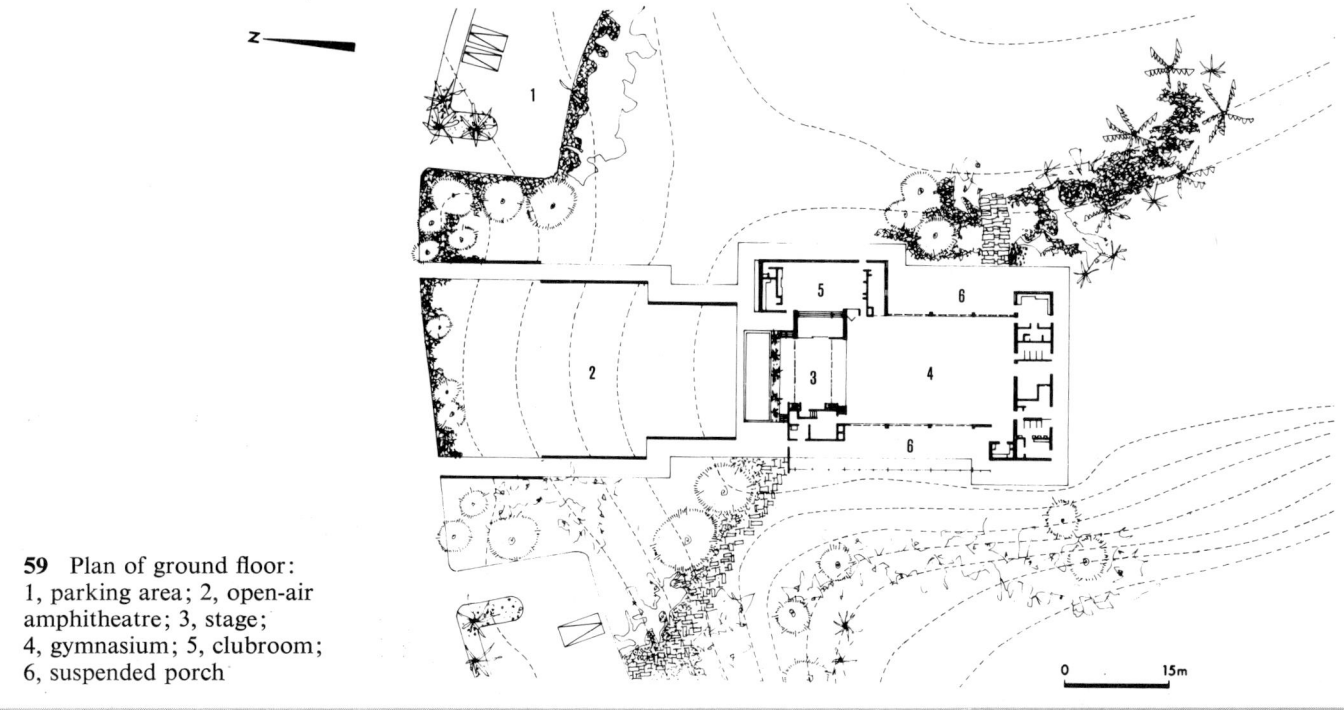

59 Plan of ground floor:
1, parking area; 2, open-air amphitheatre; 3, stage;
4, gymnasium; 5, clubroom;
6, suspended porch

60

60 Interior of gymnasium

61 The west elevation, with sun porch leading to the gymnasium via lifting doors

62-66, The Brown house, Brentwood, Los Angeles, Calif. (1955)

62 Plan of the Brown house (lower floor, above right): 1, entrance from drive; 2, living room; 3, dining area behind sliding wall; 4, kitchen; 5, cantilevered terrace; 6, garage; 7, bedroom; 8, studio; 9, swimming pool

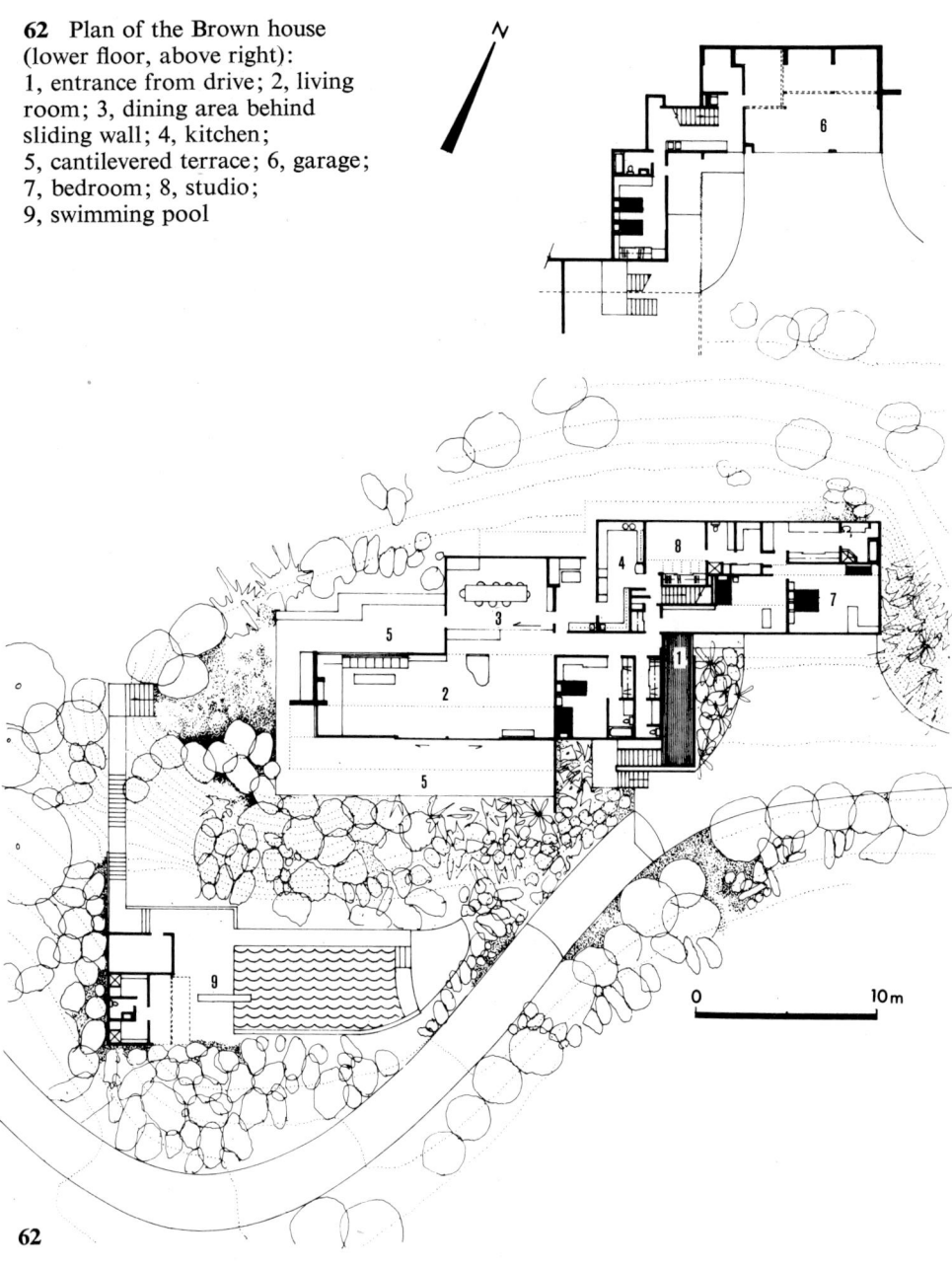

63 Corner of house overlooking approach drive

64 Access corridor above entrance steps

65 Master bedroom with garage beneath, and outrigged beam spanning drive

66 Living room and terrace, showing immense plate-glass windows

67-71, The Perkins house, Pasadena, Calif. (1955)

67 Plan of the Perkins house: 1, entrance; 2, living room; 3, studio; 4, kitchen and dining area; 5, elevated terrace; 6, car port; 7, bedroom; 8, pool

68 Access drive and steps to the entrance

69 The living room looking south-east

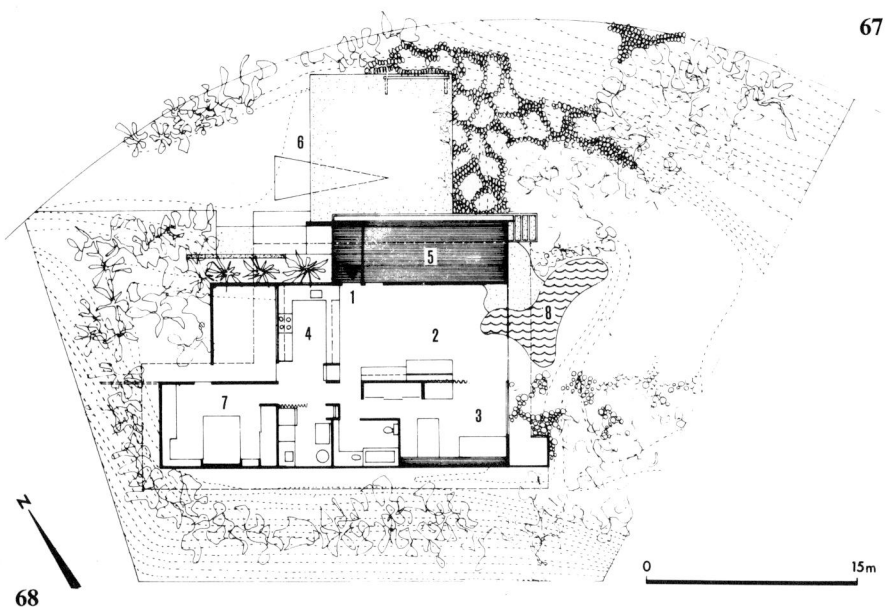

70 The transparent effect: pool enters living room, outrigger enters pool

71 Timber terrace with translucent screen concealing entrance

72-77, The Slavin house, Santa Barbara, Calif. (1957)

72 The south elevation seen from the approach road

73 Entrance and car port beneath the west wing

74 Entrance steps from car port to house

75 Extended balcony outside rumpus room

76 Site plan, showing: 1, entrance hall; 2, living and dining area; 3, study; 4, kitchen; 5, terrace; 6, garage (below bedroom); 7, bedrooms; 8, rumpus room; 9, swimming pool; 10, approach road

77 View from living and dining area towards rumpus room and balcony

73

74

75

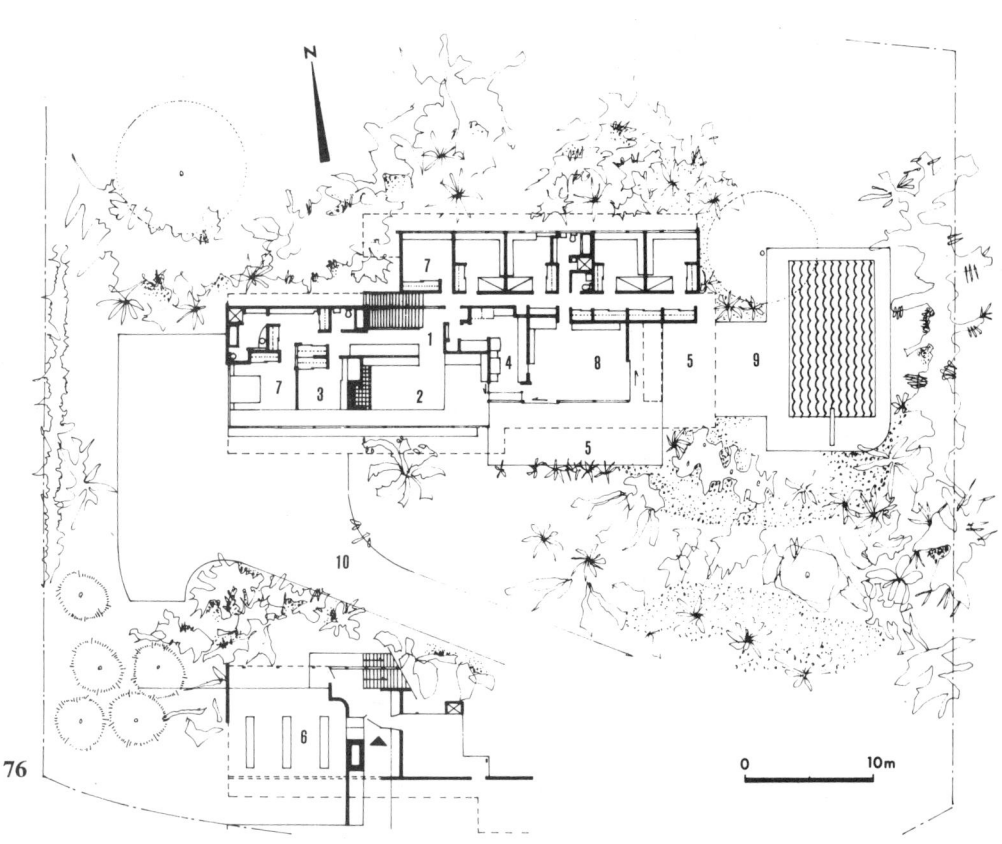

78-82, Adelphi College Library, Garden City, Long Island, N.Y. (1957-63)

78 Aluminium slatted first-floor façade and vertically coursed brick screen wall to entrance

79 The courtyard to the north of the reading area

80 Pool and fountain viewed from the spiral stair

81 Plan of the library building:
1, entrance; 2, foyer; 3, librarians' counter; 4, catalogue room; 5, bookstacks; 6, reading area; 7, offices; 8, open courtyard

82 Southern reading area with spiral stair to left and mirror to right

83-88, The Singleton house, Los Angeles, Calif. (1960)

83 Steps from drive to entrance

84 Outrigged beam projecting beyond the living room

85 The living room from the south, with a bedroom on the right

86 Butt-joined plate glass in the corner of the living room

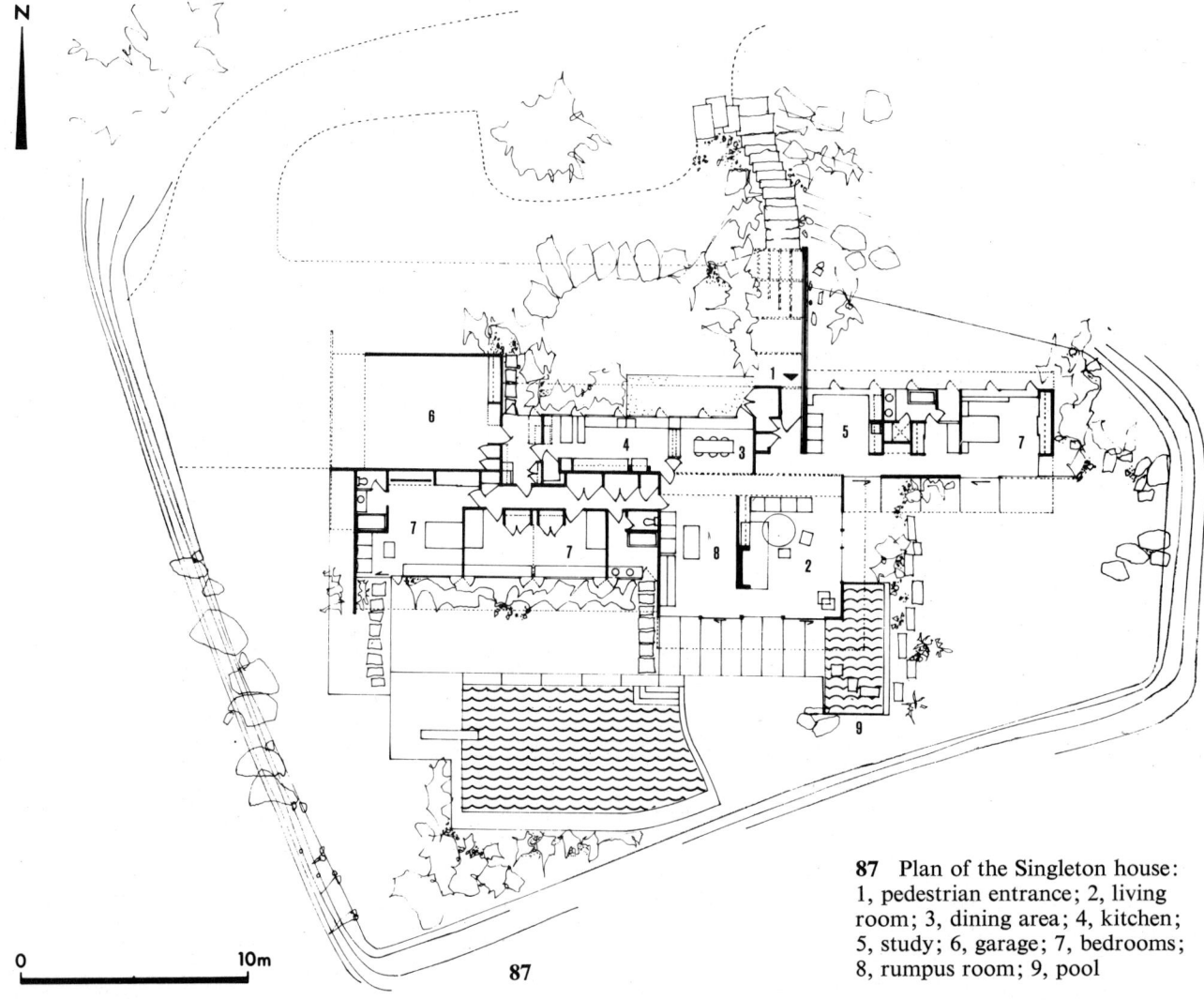

87 Plan of the Singleton house: 1, pedestrian entrance; 2, living room; 3, dining area; 4, kitchen; 5, study; 6, garage; 7, bedrooms; 8, rumpus room; 9, pool

88 The entrance hall

89-93, Garden Grove Community Church, Calif. (1962)

89 Inside the courtyard: a contrast of water, stone and steel

90 General view from the east

91

92

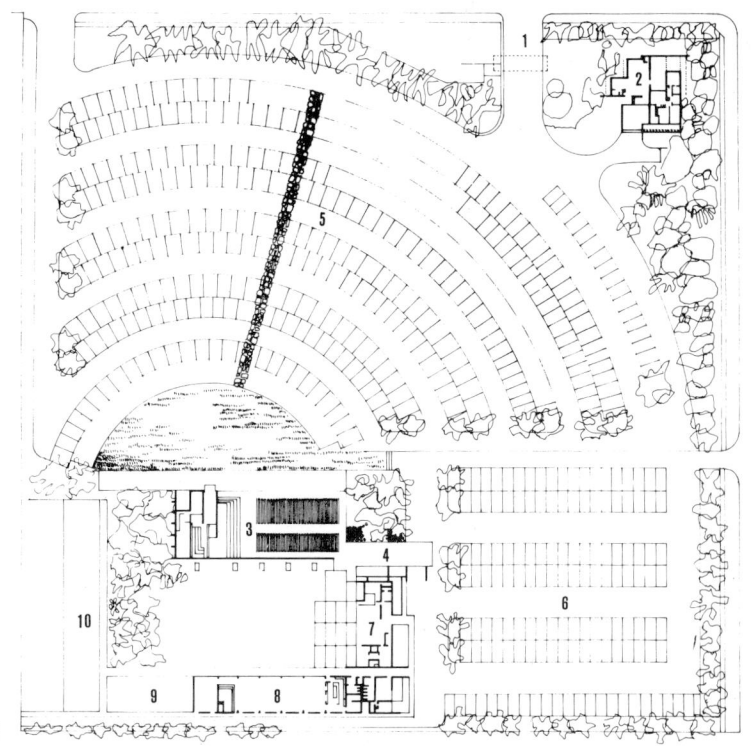

91 The moat beneath cantilevered roof on the east side

92 Interior of the church

93 Plan of the church:
1, entrance gate; 2, minister's house; 3, the church; 4, pedestrian entrance; 5, parking for drive-in congregation; 6, parking for worshippers entering church; 7, offices; 8, club room; 9, kindergarten; 10, Sunday school

**94-100, The Rados house,
San Pedro, Los Angeles, Calif. (1961)**

94 The east elevation, showing steel staircase at left leading from pool level to living and dining rooms

95 View at lower level with pool to the right

96 Plate-glass partitioning surrounding pool

95

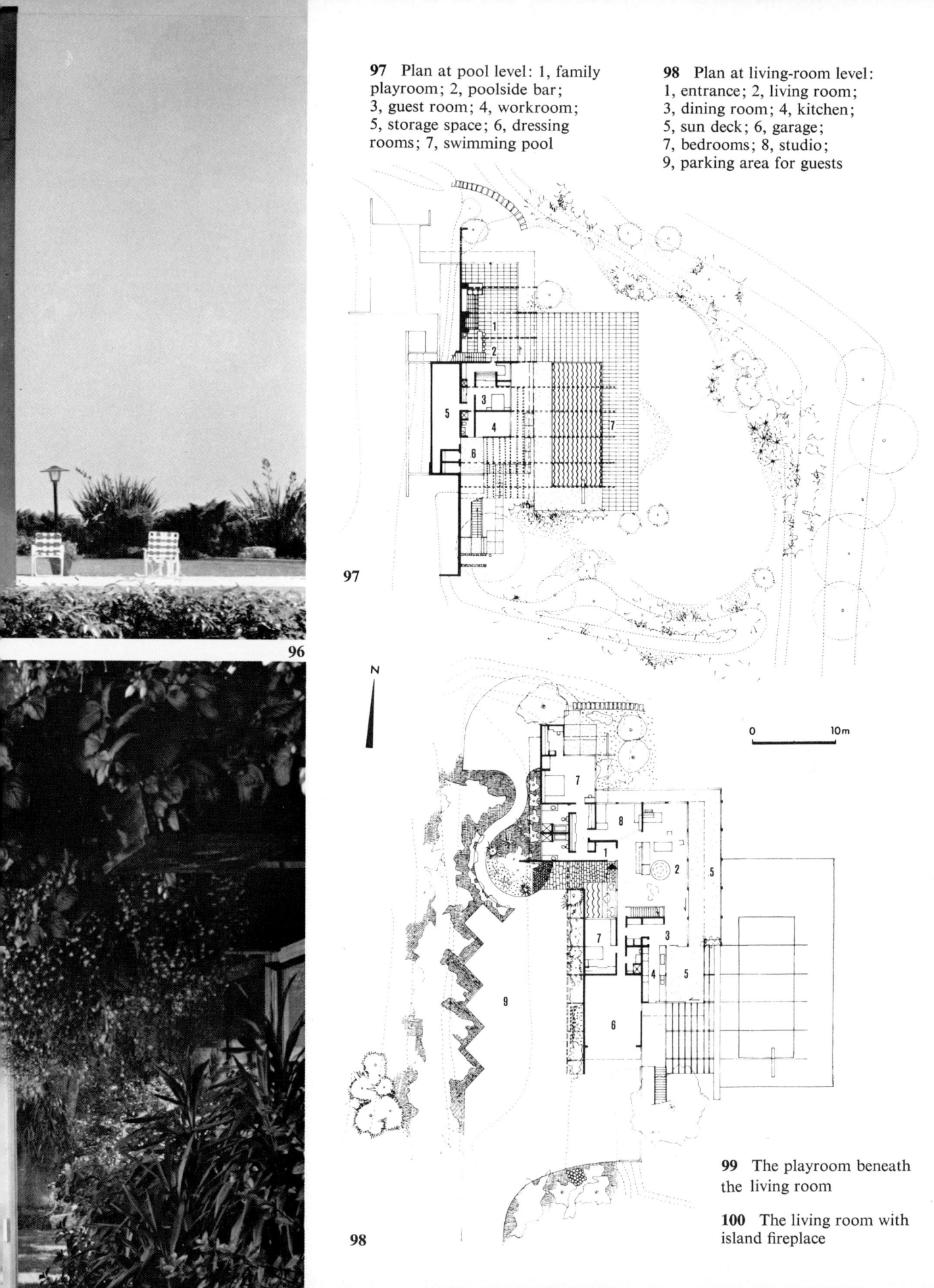

97 Plan at pool level: 1, family playroom; 2, poolside bar; 3, guest room; 4, workroom; 5, storage space; 6, dressing rooms; 7, swimming pool

98 Plan at living-room level: 1, entrance; 2, living room; 3, dining room; 4, kitchen; 5, sun deck; 6, garage; 7, bedrooms; 8, studio; 9, parking area for guests

99 The playroom beneath the living room

100 The living room with island fireplace

101-107, The Mariners Medical Arts Center, Newport Beach, Calif. (1963)

101 Plan of Mariners Medical Arts Center: 1, entrance drive; 2, covered walkways; 3, interior court; 4, reception and waiting area; 5, garages; 6, parking lot

102 East elevation seen from the parking lot

103 Entrance walkway through internal court

104 The main entrance at the end of the walkway

105 Elevation to western parking lot

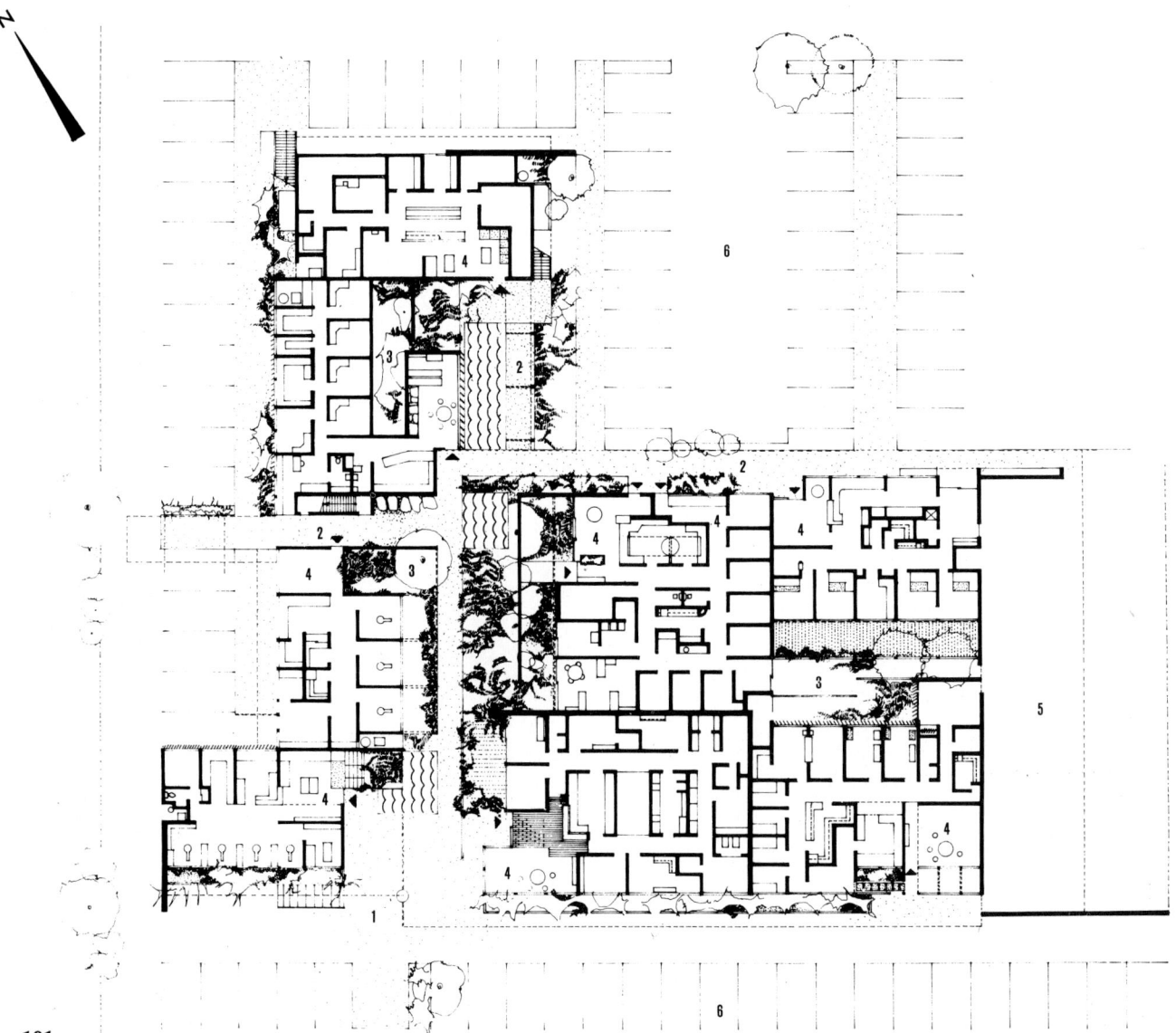

102   103

106

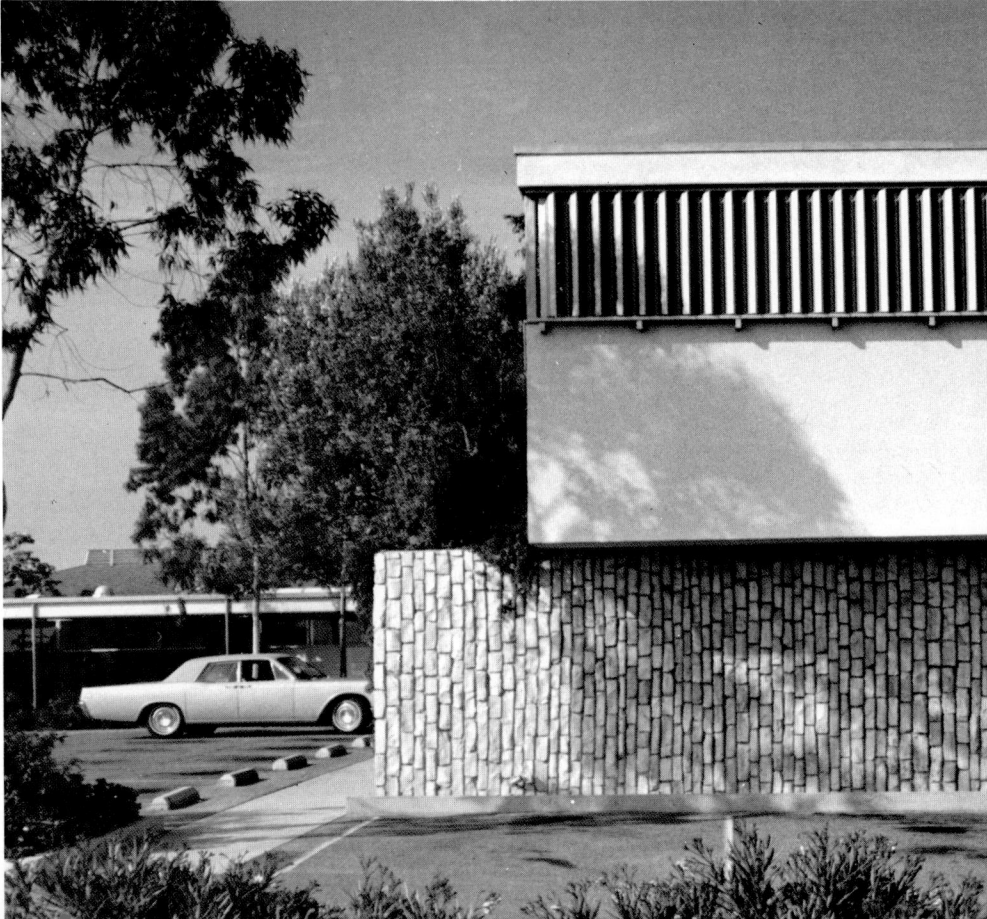

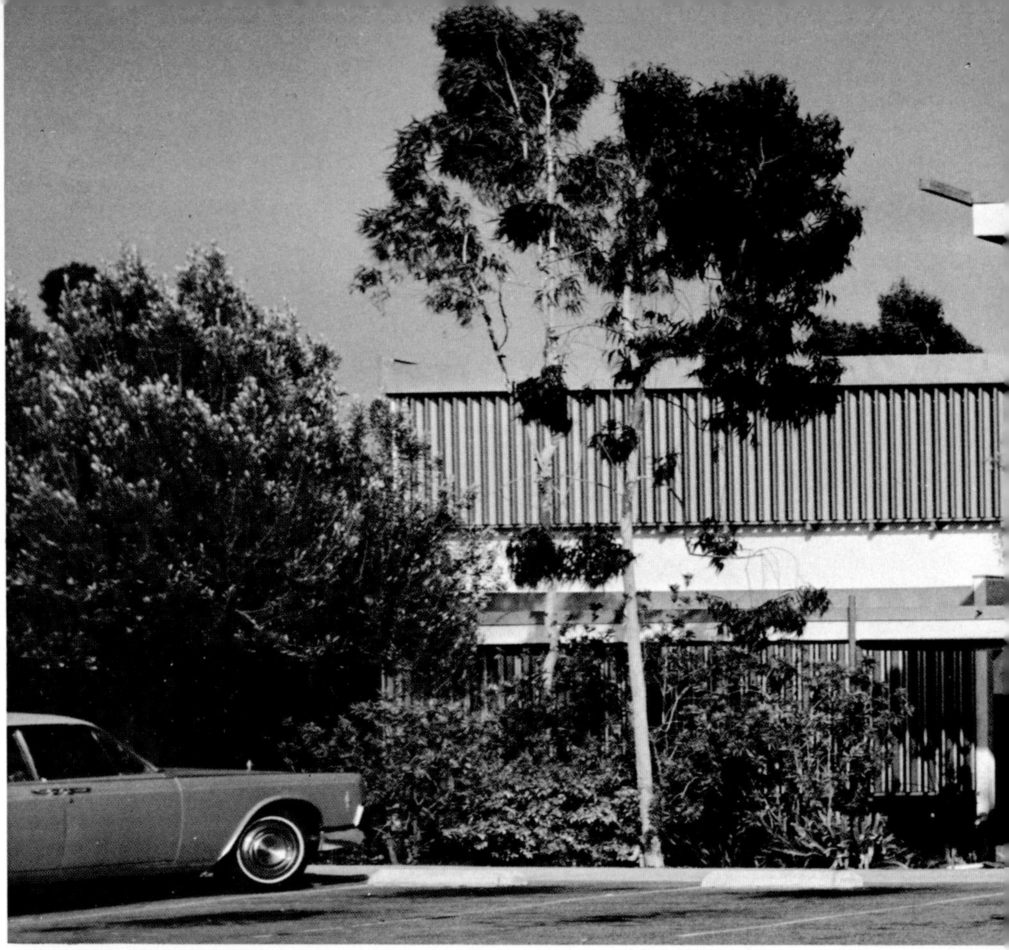

107

106 Vertical louvres to the west

107 The south elevation with vertically coursed stone wall

**108-114, The V.D.L. Research House,
Silver Lake, Los Angeles, Calif. (1933; rebuilt 1964)**

108 The approach road elevation, showing new aluminium louvres

109 Living room of new penthouse, showing rooftop pool

110 Living room of original house at ground-floor level; now used by Institute

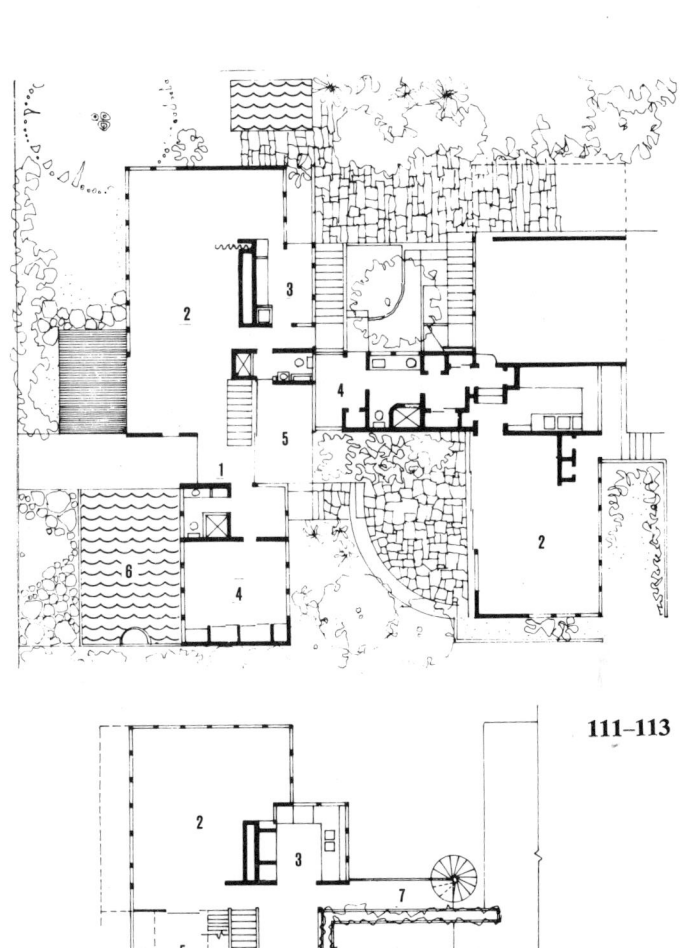
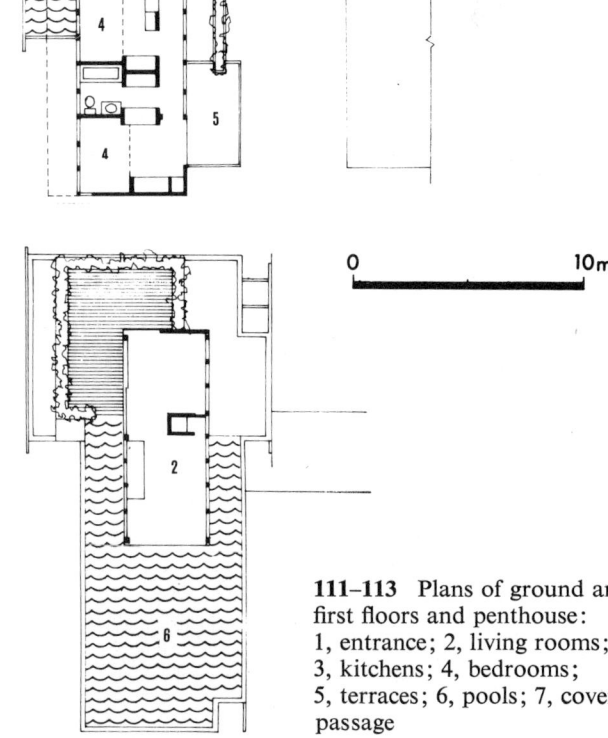

111–113 Plans of ground and first floors and penthouse: 1, entrance; 2, living rooms; 3, kitchens; 4, bedrooms; 5, terraces; 6, pools; 7, covered passage

114 First-floor living room with open, suspended stair

Notes on the plates

1–10

The Health House,
Los Angeles, California
(1929)

This comparatively large house was Neutra's first major contribution to the advanced technology of building. It secured his reputation in California and throughout the world and is still regarded by many as his most enduring work. Dr Lovell, the client, was a naturopath and for this reason Neutra always referred to the structure as the 'Health' house. The steel frame of the house was erected on concrete foundations around the rim of a steep slope down which the house descends via staircases and floor levels either cantilevered or suspended from the main structure by tension cables. The swimming pool extends out beyond the *pilotis* at the lowest level. The thin concrete walls of the house as well as its standard metal windows have been relatively well maintained by the three owners to date. Damage has, however, been caused to the lower external stair as a result of differential subsidence.

11–17

Josef von Sternberg house,
San Fernando Valley,
Los Angeles, California
(1936)

Built for a famous film director, this house was later purchased by the novelist Ayn Rand and is sometimes known by that name. Provided with a moat and roof-top pool for cooling purposes, the house is chiefly famous for the pioneer use of aluminium-faced steel sheeting to enclose the semi-circular patio to the west. This sheeting, though evident in early photographs, is now almost totally obscured from the outside by vegetation. The same aluminium-faced sheeting still forms the cladding of the external walls of the house, although much of the interior has been altered since Von Sternberg's original occupation.

18–22

The Beckstrand house,
Palos Verdes, California
(1937)

This small, single-storey house employed shop fabricated steel wall panels as part of the architect's pursuit of cheaper building materials. Apart from the use of this unprocessed aggregate, the house is simply and conventionally constructed using standard steel windows and attached steel tube supports. Some difficulty with the Californian authorities was encountered over the question of the roof design of this dwelling since the local ordinance required pitched construction. Neutra was, however, able to avoid compromise.

23–29

The Kahn house,
San Francisco, California
(1940)

This house is situated on the eastern slope of Telegraph Hill near the centre of San Francisco; its siting closely resembles that of the Health House. A four-storey steel-frame structure, the building is more rigidly planned than its forbear and possesses an eastern façade which is entirely urban in character; furthermore, there are no split floor-levels. Vertical movement between floors is by elevator or stairs. The steel windows are built to the 3ft $4\frac{1}{2}$ in. module which Neutra employed at that time.

30–35
The Nesbitt house,
Brentwood, Los Angeles,
California (1942)

Designed during wartime when there was a shortage of sophisticated building materials, the Nesbitt house employed only redwood timber, brick and glass. It marked the dawn of a new phase in Neutra's architecture, in which choice of materials became actually less important than the interpenetration of interior and exterior and the general transparency of the whole concept. Surrounded by luxuriant vegetation, the brick-floored and board-ceilinged house is divided into two areas linked by a roofed terrace. The guest house section was so designed as to make it possible to be sublet if necessary.

36–42
The Kaufmann house,
Palm Springs,
California (1945)

This 'desert house' was built for the same client as Frank Lloyd Wright's 'Fallingwater' and represents a complete change in style from its predecessor. Horizontal roofs hover over transparent glass walls and dry-jointed stone extends in an almost Miesian manner along the cruciform plan of the house. The site itself is now less remote than at the time of construction since the area is presently being developed as a resort; the famous desert aspect is itself largely a matter of photographic direction, since it is only to the west that the house looks out on to a treeless landscape.

43–48
The Tremaine house,
Santa Barbara, California
(1948)

Planned like the Kaufmann house on a cruciform pattern, the Tremaine house uses a reinforced concrete frame to create a canopy enclosing space. A regular column grid supports beams which are cantilevered beyond the screen walls to carry the lightweight flat roof. Only at the entrance, where dry-jointed stone walls are used, does the structure solidify into something approaching a conventional house. The spaces between the deep concrete roof beams are occupied by clerestory windows, with the result that the house seems remote from its roof structure. This house marks Neutra's first use of the butt-jointed plate-glass corner, here employed in the north-eastern corner of the master bedroom.

49–53
The Haefely-Moore twin
houses, Long Beach,
California (1950)

These two dwellings, built on adjacent lots at Long Beach, were designed as individual houses combined only for the purpose of presenting an integrated architectural appearance. Building regulations dictated the use of pitched roofs and in the Haefely house the roof timbers are left exposed internally in natural redwood. In the same house a large sliding glass door allows space to flow visually between the living room and the garden. Generally open-planned, the Haefely house also has an upper storey in the form of a bedroom over the garage. The Moore house allows for food preparation and cooking within the general living area. Long white-painted walls ensure privacy by the complete separation of each house and garden.

54–57
The Moore house,
Ojai, California
(1952)

One of Neutra's most famous houses, the Moore house is sited in the sub-tropical Ojai valley surrounded by orange groves and relatively close mountains; the owner's land extends over thirty acres. The building itself consists of a main house and a guest house linked by a path of stone pavings; this path is also used to cross the pool which surrounds the living room on two sides and also provides reflections of the mountains as well as being a source of water for irrigation purposes. The living area is itself almost completely glazed and the slim flat roof is carried on outrigged beams whose columns actually descend into the pool. Butt-jointed plate glass is used in living and bedroom areas.

58–61
Eagle Rock Playground
Club House, Los Angeles,
California (1953)

Housing a young people's recreation centre, this structure stands on high ground in a public park. Flexibility in the use of available space as well as integration of interior and exterior by means of transparent walls were the principal features of the design. The provision of an outdoor amphitheatre and the use of wide lifting doors greatly expand the seating capacity. The structure employs a steel frame with brick infill panels, but the porch roof is suspended on steel hangers in a manner similar to the balconies of the Health House of 1929.

62–66
The Brown house,
Brentwood, Los Angeles,
California (1955)

Built on a precipitous and extremely difficult site, this house was designed for an elderly couple with many interests including experimental theatre—for which purpose the large living room was intended to be adapted when necessary. Approached from below, the house is placed in a typical position along the rim of the hill with a fine view of the Pacific in the distance. A wide eaves overhang to the south incorporates external light fittings designed to remove interior glare at night so that the view can be enjoyed. The immense plate-glass windows to the south were as large as calculated wind forces would permit. A long outrigged beam straddles the entrance drive.

67–71
The Perkins house,
Pasadena, California
(1955)

This small and relatively cheap house carries the Neutras' principle of transparency and indeterminacy of enclosure to great extremes. The pool to the east of the living room actually penetrates into the room itself, passing beneath a full-height plate-glass wall. The transparent effect thus created is enhanced by the use of an outrigged beam carried by a column itself emerging from the pool. As a result it is difficult from the inside to determine the exact line separating interior from exterior. The house is built on a sloping site which enables the entrance to be located above the car port and access drive.

72–77
The Slavin house,
Santa Barbara,
California (1957)

This timber-and-steel framed house overlooking the shores of the Pacific stands parallel to the slope of the site. Virtually the entire southern wall is glazed and a narrow balcony cantilevered on timber beams is provided on the exterior for window cleaning. The planning of the house, which was intended for a large family, involves a central kitchen capable of serving a meal counter, a formal dining area, and the family rumpus room (which is the largest room in the house). Entry is gained by passing beneath the western end of the building and climbing a staircase to the living room. This staircase has a service stair alongside and the two are separated by a plate-glass partition.

78–82
Adelphi College Library,
Garden City, Long Island,
New York (1957–63)

Employing a vertical aluminium-slatted façade to the south with a single-storey vertically coursed brick screen wall to the entrance running beneath it, the Adelphi College Library represents a much truncated version of the original project which was to have featured a 'space-time gateway' in the form of a hollow globe portraying visually and via teletype the sources and subjects of news throughout the world. This feature was abandoned before construction and the entrance now boasts a spiral stair leading to the first floor, which is faced by a mirror wall. The concrete-framed building is built to a 22 ft 6 in. grid to allow flexibility in the positioning of library stacks.

83–88
The Singleton house,
Los Angeles, California
(1960)

A timber-and-steel house in the tradition of the Tremaine and Perkins houses, this building incorporates all the techniques the Neutras developed for integrating interior and exterior. Outrigged beams for *trompe l'oeil* effect, plate glass from floor to ceiling, and a reflecting pool. Surrounded as it is by trees, the house nonetheless possesses spectacular views to the south towards the Santa Monica mountains, and overlooks the entire city of Los Angeles and the Pacific coast. Butt-jointed glass is used on the corner of the living room, together with profiled timber ceilings and a natural-stone fireplace.

89–93
Garden Grove Community
Church, California
(1962)

This extraordinary structure incorporates a radial drive-in amphitheatre facing a pulpit, a 24-hour telephone service—dial 'hope'—and a thirteenth-storey 'chapel in the sky' capable of accommodating over 130 persons (this was added in 1967). The architect's brief was to create a religious structure of significance and permanence which would stand out among the secular sprawl of the community of Garden Grove. Reinforced concrete was used for the structural frame and natural stone for some walls. A moat surrounds the entire building which boasts administrative offices as well as a sculptural tower so designed that from certain positions symbolic shadows are cast by the sun.

94–100
The Rados house,
San Pedro, Los Angeles,
California (1961)

Built for a wealthy boatbuilding family, this house incorporates numerous marine structural techniques, including the use of boat-varnish on all exposed timber. An exterior sun deck with a glass-walled living room, which incorporates an island fireplace with stainless hood and flue, gives on to an internal courtyard with pool, plants and glazed walls. A welded steel tube staircase of nautical appearance links the main living level with the pool area below.

101–107
The Mariners Medical Arts Center, Newport Beach, California (1963)

For the most part a single-storey building, the Medical Arts Center encloses an internal garden with pool and luxuriant planting, its two-storey elements are cunningly interwoven with covered walkways; alternate horizontal-and vertical-louvred aluminium cladding presents an entirely bland exterior with all openings toward the centre. A large number of individual surgeries and consulting rooms are incorporated into the Center.

108–114
The V.D.L. Research House, Silver Lake, Los Angeles, California (1933, rebuilt 1964 with the help of Dion Neutra)

This house was first built in 1933 as the architect's own house and was financed by the Dutch industrialist Van Der Leeuw, after whom it was named. It boasted numerous materials and techniques which were at that time revolutionary in terms of housing applications, including chipboard, steel-sash windows, plate glass, custom-made sliding doors, stove-enamelled metal wall facings and a suspended, arched concrete floor slab.

When rebuilt in 1964, after a fire which almost completely destroyed the old building, the house featured tall external louvres to take the place of the shade trees destroyed in the fire, a penthouse, a pool at roof-level, and increased use of reflective glass and mirrors. The ground floor serves as the headquarters of the Richard J. Neutra Institute, founded to carry on some of the Neutra ideals.

Chronological list: projects and events

Unless otherwise stated all buildings and projects listed after 1923 are in California; an asterisk indicates a project in partnership with Robert Alexander

1892 Born in Vienna, Austria
1914–17 Served as artillery officer in Imperial Austrian army
1917 Graduated from Technische Hochschule, Vienna
1922 Married Dione Niedermann of Zurich
1923 With Erich Mendelsohn won first prize in competition for Business Centre, Haifa (project not executed); emigrated to United States
1924 Worked as a draughtsman in the offices of Holabird and Roche, Chicago
1925 With Frank Lloyd Wright at Taliesin North
1926 With Rudolph Schindler in Los Angeles; opens own office
1926–30 'Rush City Reformed' (project)
1927 Jardinette Apartments, Los Angeles; League of Nations Secretariat competition entry (with Schindler)
1929 Lovell house ('Health House'), Los Angeles
1933 Architect's own house (V.D.L. Research House), Los Angeles; rebuilt 1964
1935 Beard House, Altadena; Corona Avenue School, Bell, Los Angeles
1936 Plywood Model House; Von Sternberg house (Ayn Rand house), San Fernando Valley, Los Angeles; California Military Academy, Los Angeles
1937 Beckstrand house, Palos Verdes
1938 Strathmore Apartments, Westwood, Los Angeles; Emerson Junior High School, Westwood, Los Angeles
1939 National Youth Administration Centers, Sacramento and San Luis Obispo; Amity Village, Compton (mutual housing development project)
1940 Kahn house, San Francisco
1941 Avion Village, Texas

1942 Nesbitt house, Brentwood, Los Angeles; Channel Heights, San Pedro (Federal Public Housing development by Richard and Dion Neutra); Kelton Apartments, Westwood, Los Angeles
1944 Rural school buildings and health centres, Puerto Rico; urban schools, health centres and hospitals, Puerto Rico
1946 Kaufmann house (Desert House), Palm Springs
1948 Tremaine house, Santa Barbara; Aloe Medical Supply Building, Los Angeles; Holiday house, Malibu
1949 Partnership with Robert Alexander (joint projects designated by asterisk)
1950 *Urban redevelopment plan for Sacramento (project)
1950–53 *Elysian Park Heights (urban redevelopment for Los Angeles Housing Authority; project); Eagle Rock Playground Club House, Los Angeles
1951 Hinds house, Los Angeles; Northwestern Mutual Fire Insurance Building, Los Angeles
1952 Moore house, Ojai
1953 Kester Avenue Elementary School, Los Angeles
1954 *Child Guidance Clinic, Los Angeles; *Business Education Building, Orange Coast College, Costa Mesa
1955 Medical Center, San Bernardino, Los Angeles; *Science Building and Auditorium, St John's College, Annapolis, Md
1956 Gemological Institute of America, Brentwood, Los Angeles
1957 *Science Building, Speech, Arts and Music Auditorium and sports facilities, Orange Coast College, Costa Mesa; *Miramar Chapel, La Jolla; *Alamitos Intermediate School, Garden Grove
1958 *Riviera Methodist Church, Redondo Beach; *Elementary Training School, University of California at Los Angeles
1959 Competition for Düsseldorf theatre, Germany (project); *Museum of Natural History and Planetarium, Dayton, Ohio
1960 Singleton house, Los Angeles
1962 Garden Grove Community Church
1963 *Adelphi College library building, Garden City, Long Island, N.Y.; *United States Embassy, Karachi, Pakistan; *Mariners Medical Arts Center, Newport Beach; *Lincoln Memorial Museum Gettysburg, Pennsylvania; V.D.L. Research House largely destroyed by fire (rebuilt 1964)
1964 *Hall of Records, Los Angeles; *Richard J. Neutra Elementary School, Lemoore
1965 Friedland house, Philadelphia, Pennsylvania
1966 Bucerius house, Navegna, Switzerland
1967 'Tower of Hope' added to Garden Grove Church
1969 Orange County Courthouse, Santa Ana
1970 Died 16 April, in Wuppertal, West Germany

Select bibliography

Boesiger, W., ed., *Richard Neutra, Buildings and Projects*: vol. I (1923–50), 1954; vol. II (1950–60), 1960; vol. III (1961–66), 1966, all London and New York
McCoy, Esther, *Richard Neutra*, New York, 1960, and London, 1961
Neutra, Richard, *Wie Baut Amerika*, Stuttgart, 1927; *Mysteries and Realities of the Site*, New York, 1951; *Survival Through Design*, Oxford and New York, 1954 (paperback edition, 1969)
Zevi, Bruno, *Richard Neutra*, Milan, 1954

Journals

L'architecture d'aujourd'hui, June 1948; special issue on Neutra
L'architettura, 181, Rome, November 1970; special obituary issue on Neutra
Vitrum, 131, May/June 1962; special issue on Neutra

Index

Numbers in italics refer to the plates

Adelphi College Library (Garden City, Long Island, N.Y.) 128, *78–82*
Alexander, Robert 17
Ammann, Gustav 11
Architectural League of New York 14

Beard house (Altadena, Calif.) 15
Beckstrand house (Palos Verdes, Calif.) 15, 125, *18–22*
'Biorealism' 16, 17
Brown house (Los Angeles, Calif.) 127, *62–66*

California Military Academy (Los Angeles) 15
Chicago Tribune building 11
Congrès Internationaux d'Architecture Moderne (CIAM) 13

Diatomaceous earth 15, 125

Eagle Rock Playground Club House (Los Angeles, Calif.) 127, *58–61*
Elysian Park redevelopment (Los Angeles; project) 17

Federal Housing Administration 16
Fuller, Buckminster 15

Garden Grove Community Church (Calif.) 128, *89–93*
Guam, master plan for 17

Haefely-Moore houses (Long Beach, Calif.) 126, *49–53*
Health House (Los Angeles, Calif.) 12, 13, 125, 127, *1–10*

Hinchman and Grillis (Detroit) 12
Holabird and Roche (Chicago) 12

industrialized building methods 15

Jardinette Apartment building (Los Angeles, Calif.) 12

Kahn house (San Francisco, Calif.) 125, *23–29*
Kaufmann house (Palm Springs, Calif.) 126, *36–42*

Le Corbusier 9, 14
Lemoore, Calif.: Richard J. Neutra School 17
Lincoln Memorial Museum (Gettysburg, Pa) 17
Loos, Adolf 10, 11, 16
Lovell house (Los Angeles, Calif.) *see* Health House

Mariners Medical Arts Center (Newport Beach, Calif.) 129, *101–107*
Mendelsohn, Erich 11, 12
Moore house (Ojai valley, Calif.) 17, 127, *54–57*
Moore house (Long Beach, Calif.) *see* Haefely-Moore houses

Nesbitt house (Los Angeles, Calif.) 14, 16, 126, *30–35*
Neutra, Dion 15, 17

'One Plus Two' (project) 15
'Operation Breakthrough' (U.S.A.) 15

Perkins house (Pasadena, Calif.) 127, *67–71*

prefabrication 12–13, 15

Rados house (Los Angeles, Calif.) 128–9, *94–100*
Rand, Ayn, house (Los Angeles) *see* Sternberg house
Rush City Reformed (project) 12, 14

Schindler, Rudolph 11, 12, 13
Singleton house (Los Angeles, Calif.) 128, *83–88*
Slavin house (Santa Barbara, Calif.) 127, *72–77*
Sternberg, Josef von, house (Los Angeles, Calif.) 15, 125, *11–17*

Sullivan, Louis 12

'Technocracy' 14, 19*n*
Tremaine house (Santa Barbara, Calif.) 126, *43–48*

U.S. Embassy building (Karachi, Pakistan) 17

Van Der Leeuw, C.H. 13, 129
V.D.L. Research House (Los Angeles, Calif.) 13, 15, 129, *108–114*

Wagner, Otto 10
Wright, Frank Lloyd 11, 12, 13, 14, 126